Stanley Gibb

COLLE

Irish

STAMPS

STANLEY GIBBONS LTD
London and Ringwood

By Appointment to
Her Majesty The Queen,
Stanley Gibbons Ltd., London,
Philatelists

Published by **Stanley Gibbons Publications**
Editorial, Sales Offices and Distribution Centre:
5 Parkside, Christchurch Road, Ringwood,
Hants BH24 3SH

FIRST EDITION (1999)

ISBN: 0-85259-479-8

© Stanley Gibbons Ltd 1999

Item No. 0290 (99)

Text assembled and Printed in Great Britain by
Black Bear Press Limited, Cambridge.

COLLECT IRISH STAMPS

For many years collectors have been asking us to provide a checklist covering the stamps of Ireland as a companion to our established *Collect British Stamps* and *Collect Channel Islands and Isle of Man Stamps*. This has now become possible as part of the major project to update the production methods used for the Stanley Gibbons catalogues.

The listings in this catalogue have been taken from the *Part 1 Catalogue* (2000 Edition) and extended to cover new issues up to the "Millennium Football Team" series issued on 17 August 1999. Prices for commemorative First Day Covers, Year Packs and Year Books will be found at the end of the catalogue after the listing of Stamp Booklets. As an added bonus, all stamp illustrations are shown in colour, taken from the comprehensive illustration database which is currently being assembled for use throughout the catalogue range.

Stamps from Ireland have always been widely collected, but in recent years their popularity has increased by the inclusion of interesting thematic issues within restrained new issue programmes. It is our hope that this first edition will provide a handy listing to encourage more collectors to *Collect Irish Stamps*.

Scope. *Collect Irish Stamps* comprises:
- All stamps with different watermark (*wmk*) or perforation (*perf*)
- Phosphor issues
- Commemorative First Day Covers (prices at end of listing)
- Year Packs (prices at end of listing)
- Post Office Year Books (prices at end of listing)
- Postage Due Stamps
- Errors and Varieties
- Stamp Booklets

Layout. Stamps are set out chronologically by date of issue. In the catalogue lists the first numeral is the Stanley Gibbons catalogue number, the black (boldface) numeral alongside is the type number referring to the respective illustration. A blank in this column implies that the number immediately above is repeated. The denomination and colour of the stamp are then shown. Before February 1971 Irish currency was:

£1 = 20s   One pound = twenty shillings and

1s = 12d   One shilling = twelve pence.

Upon decimalisation this became:

£1 = 100p   One pound = one hundred (new) pence.

The catalogue list shows two price columns. The left-hand is for unused stamps and the right-hand for used.

Our method of indicating prices is: Numerals for pence, e.g. 10 denotes 10p (10 pence). Numerals for pounds and pence, e.g. 4·25 (4 pounds and 25 pence). For £100 and above, prices are in whole pounds and so include the £ sign and omit the zeros for pence.

Colour illustrations. The colour illustrations of stamps are intended as a guide only; they may differ in shade from the originals.

Size of illustrations. To comply with Post Office regulations stamp illustrations are three-quarters linear size. Separate illustrations of surcharges, overprints and watermarks are actual size.

Prices. Prices quoted in this catalogue are our selling prices in sterling currency at the time the book went to press. They are for stamps in fine condition; in issues where condition varies we may ask more for the superb and less for the sub-standard. The unused prices for stamps from 1922 until 1935 are for lightly hinged examples.

Unused prices for issues since 1935 are for unmounted mint (though when not available unmounted, mounted stamps are often supplied at a lower price). Prices for used stamps refer to postally used examples. All prices are subject to change without prior notice and we give no guarantee to supply all stamps priced, since it is not possible to keep every catalogued item in stock. Individual low value stamps sold at 399, Strand are liable to an additional handling charge. Commemorative issues may, at times, only be available in complete sets.

In the price columns:
† = Does not exist.
(—) or blank = Exists, or may exist, but price cannot be quoted.

Perforations. The "perforation" is the number of holes in a length of 2 cm. as measured by the Gibbons *Instanta* gauge. The stamp is viewed against a dark background with the transparent gauge put on top of it. Perforations are quoted to the nearest half. Stamps without perforation are termed "imperforate".

Se-tenant combinations. *Se-tenant* means "joined together". Some sets include stamps in different designs arranged *se-tenant* as pairs, blocks or strips and these are often collected unsevered as issued. Where such combinations exist the stamps are priced mint as singles or complete combinations. The set price for mint refers to the unsevered combination plus singles of any other values in the set. The used set price is for single stamps of all values.

Commemorative First Day Covers. Prices for First Day Covers are for complete sets used on plain covers (Nos. 89 to 148) or on special covers (Nos. 149/51 onwards) the stamps of which are cancelled with ordinary operational postmarks (1929–1949) or by "First Day of Issue" postmarks (1950 onwards). Prices for First Day Covers will be found on page 60.

Year Packs and Year Books. Annual Year Packs were introduced in 1976. From 1989 onwards Year Books were also produced. Prices for these items will be found on page 61.

Catalogue numbers used. The checklist uses the same catalogue numbers as the Stanley Gibbons *Part 1 Catalogue*, 2000 Edition.

Latest issue date for stamps recorded in this edition is 17 August 1999.

STANLEY GIBBONS LTD

Head Office: 399 Strand, London WC2R 0LX.

Auction Room and Specialist Stamp Departments. Open Monday–Friday 9.30 a.m. to 5 p.m. **Shop.** Open Monday to Friday 8.30 a.m. to 6 p.m. and Saturday 9.30 a.m. to 5.30 p.m.

Telephone: 020 7836 8444 for all departments.
E-mail: stamps@stangiblondon.demon.co.uk
Website: www.stangib.com

Stanley Gibbons Publications:
5 Parkside, Christchurch Road,
Ringwood, Hants BH24 3SH
Telephone: 01425 472363
Publications Mail Order
FREEPHONE: 0800 611622
E-mail: info@stangib.demon.co.uk

Ireland

1922 12 pence (d) = 1 shilling;
20 shillings = 1 pound
1971 100 (new) pence = 1 pound

<table>
<tr><td colspan="2">PRICES FOR STAMPS ON COVER TO 1945</td></tr>
<tr><td>Nos. 1/15</td><td>from × 5</td></tr>
<tr><td>Nos. 17/21</td><td>from × 3</td></tr>
<tr><td>Nos. 26/9a</td><td>from × 5</td></tr>
<tr><td>Nos. 30/43</td><td>from × 4</td></tr>
<tr><td>Nos. 44/6</td><td></td></tr>
<tr><td>Nos. 47/63</td><td>from × 5</td></tr>
<tr><td>Nos. 64/6</td><td>from × 3</td></tr>
<tr><td>Nos. 67/70</td><td>from × 6</td></tr>
<tr><td>Nos. 71/82</td><td>from × 2</td></tr>
<tr><td>Nos. 83/8</td><td>from × 3</td></tr>
<tr><td>Nos. 89/98</td><td>from × 2</td></tr>
<tr><td>Nos. 99/104</td><td>from × 3</td></tr>
<tr><td>Nos. 105/37</td><td>from × 2</td></tr>
<tr><td>Nos. D1/4</td><td>from × 7</td></tr>
<tr><td>Nos. D5/14</td><td>from × 6</td></tr>
</table>

PROVISIONAL GOVERNMENT

16 January—6 December 1922

Stamps of Great Britain overprinted.

(1)

(2)

(3)

("Provisional Government of Ireland, 1922")

1922 (17 Feb–July). *Stamps of Great Britain overprinted in black.*

(a) With T **1**, *by Dollard Printing Co. Ltd. Optd in black**

1	¹/₂d. green	..	..	..	..	85	40
	a. Opt inverted	..	..	..	£400	£550
2	1d. scarlet	..	..	..	..	1·25	35
	a. Opt inverted	..	..	..	£250	£300
	b. Opt double, both inverted, one albino		£350	
	c. Opt double	..	..	..	..	÷	—
	w. Wmk inverted	..	..	..	—	£150
3	1d. carmine-red	..	..	..	2·25	50
4	2¹/₂d. bright blue	..	..	..	1·50	4·50
	a. Red opt (1 Apr)	..	..	..	85	3·25
5	3d. bluish violet	..	..	..	4·00	3·75
6	4d. grey-green	..	..	..	3·25	9·50
	a. Red opt (1 Apr)	..	..	..	8·00	15·00
	b. Carmine opt (July)	..	..	40·00	65·00
7	5d. yellow-brown	..	..	..	3·75	8·50
	x. Wmk reversed	..	..	..	—	£200

8	9d. agate	..	..	..	..	10·00	20·00
	a. Opt double, one albino	..	..		
	b. Red opt (1 Apr)	..	..	..	13·00	17·00
	c. Carmine opt (July)	..	..	80·00	85·00
9	10d. turquoise-blue	..	..	..	8·00	35·00
1/9		..	..	..	*Set of* 8	28·00	70·00

*All values except 2¹/₂d. and 4d. are known with greyish black overprint, but these are difficult to distinguish.

The carmine overprints on the 4d. and 9d. may have been produced by Alex Thom & Co. Ltd. There was a further overprinting of the 2¹/₂d. at the same time, but this is difficult to distinguish.

The ¹/₂d. with red overprint is a trial or proof printing (*Price* £150).

Bogus inverted T **1** overprints exist on the 2d., 4d., 9d and 1s. values.

(b) With T **2**, *by Alex Thom & Co Ltd.*

10	1¹/₂d. red-brown	..	..	..	..	1·25	85
	a. Error. "PENCF"	..	..	..	£350	£275
	w. Wmk inverted	..	..	..	—	£120
	x. Wmk reversed	..	..	..	—	£120
12	2d. orange (Die I)	..	..	..	2·25	50
	a. Opt inverted	..	..	..	£180	£250
	w. Wmk inverted	..	..	..	—	£100
	x. Wmk reversed	..	..	..	—	£120
13	2d. orange (Die II)	..	..	..	2·00	50
	a. Opt inverted	..	..	..	£300	£400
	w. Wmk inverted	..	..	..	—	£120
14	6d. reddish purple (*chalk-surfaced paper*)		11·00	8·00
15	1s. bistre-brown	..	..	..	11·00	9·00
10/15		..	..	..	*Set of* 5	24·00	20·00

Varieties occur throughout the T **2** overprint in the relative positions of the lines of the overprint, the "R" of "Rialtas" being over either the "Se" or "S" of "Sealadac" or intermediately.

(c) With T **3** *by Dollard Printing House Ltd*

17	2s. 6d. chocolate-brown	..	..	35·00	65·00
18	2s. 6d. reddish brown	..	..	50·00	75·00
19	5s. rose-red	..	..	..	60·00	£120
21	10s. dull grey-blue	..	..	..	£120	£250
17/21		..	..	*Set of* 3	£190	£400

1922 (19 June–Aug). *Optd as T **2**, in black, by Harrison & Sons, for use in horiz and vert coils.*

26	¹/₂d. green	..	..	..	..	2·25	10·00
27	1d. scarlet	..	..	..	..	2·50	6·00
28	1¹/₂d. red-brown (21.6)	..	..	..	4·00	32·00
29	2d. bright orange (Die I)	..	..	18·00	50·00
29a	2d. bright orange (Die II) (August)	..	19·00	25·00
	ay. Wmk inverted and reversed	..	..	—	£200
26/9a		..	..	*Set of* 5	40·00	90·00

The Harrison overprint measures 15×17 mm (maximum) against the 14¹/₂×16 mm of T **2** (Thom printing) and is a much bolder black than the latter, while the individual letters are taller, the "i" of "Rialtas" being specially outstanding as it extends below the foot of the "R".

The "R" of "Rialtas" is always over the "Se" of "Sealadac".

1922. *Optd by Thom.*

(a) As T **2** *but bolder, in dull to shiny blue-black or red* (June–Nov)

30	¹/₂d. green	..	..	..	..	1·75	80
31	1d. scarlet	..	..	..	..	1·00	50
	a. "Q" for "O" (No. 357ab)	..	£1200	£1100
	b. Reversed "Q" for "O" (No. 357ac)	£350	£250
32	1¹/₂d. red-brown	..	..	..	3·25	3·25
33	2d. orange (Die I)	..	..	..	17·00	2·00
34	2d. orange (Die II)	..	..	..	2·50	50
	y. Wmk inverted and reversed	..	..	£120	£120
35	2¹/₂d. blue (R.)	..	..	..	6·00	18·00
36	3d. violet	..	..	..	..	2·25	2·00
	y. Wmk inverted and reversed	..	..	75·00	75·00
37	4d. grey-green (R.)	..	..	..	3·00	4·50

38	5d. yellow-brown		4·00	8·50
39	6d. reddish purple (*chalk-surfaced paper*)		7·50	3·00
	w. Wmk inverted		75·00	50·00
40	9d. agate (R.)		12·00	15·00
41	9d. olive-green (R.)		4·75	30·00
42	10d. turquoise-blue		25·00	48·00
43	1s. bistre-brown		8·50	11·00
30/43		Set of 14	80·00	£130

Both 2d. stamps exist with the overprint inverted but there remains some doubt as to whether they were issued.

These Thom printings are distinguishable from the Harrison printings by the size of the overprint, and from the previous Thom printings by the intensity and colour of the overprint, the latter being best seen when the stamp is looked through with a strong light behind it.

(*b*) As with T *3, but bolder, in shiny blue-black* (Oct–Dec)
44	2s. 6d. chocolate-brown		£180	£250
45	5s. rose-red		£170	£275
46	10s. dull grey-blue		£850	£1000
44/6		Set of 3	£1100	£1400

The above differ from Nos. 17/21 not only in the bolder impression and colour of the ink but also in the "h" and "é" of "héireann" which are closer together and horizontally aligned.

(4)　　　　　(5 Wide date)
　　　　　　("Irish Free State 1922")

1922 (21 Nov–Dec). *Optd by Thom with T 4 (wider setting) in shiny blue-black.*
47	½d. green		1·00	1·75
	a. Opt in jet-black		£100	90·00
48	1d. scarlet		3·75	2·50
49	1½d. red-brown (4 December)		3·00	9·00
50	2d. orange (Die II)		9·00	6·50
51	1s. olive-bistre (4 December)		45·00	48·00
47/51		Set of 5	55·00	60·00

The overprint T 4 measures 15³/₄×16 mm (maximum).

IRISH FREE STATE
6 December 1922—29 December 1937

1922 (Dec)–**23.** *Stamps of Great Britain.*

(*a*) *Optd by Thom with T 5, in dull to shiny blue-black or red*
52	½d. green		1·00	30
	a. No accent in "Saorstat"		£1000	£900
	b. Accent inserted by hand		85·00	95·00
53	1d. scarlet		75	40
	aa. No accent in "Saorstat"		£7000	£5000
	a. No accent and final "t" missing		£6000	£4500
	b. Accent inserted by hand		£130	£150
	c. Accent and "t" inserted		£225	£250
	d. Reversed "Q" for "O" (No. 357ac)		£300	£250
54	1½d. red-brown		3·25	8·50
55	2d. orange (Die II)		1·00	1·50
56	2½d. bright blue (R.) (6.1.23)		6·00	7·00
	a. No accent		£140	£170
57	3d. bluish violet (6.1.23)		3·50	11·00
	a. No accent		£250	£275
58	4d. grey-green (R.) (16.1.23)		2·75	5·50
	a. No accent		£150	£170
59	5d. yellow-brown		3·25	4·75
60	6d. reddish purple (*chalk-surfaced paper*)		2·00	2·00
	a. Accent inserted by hand		£700	£700
	y. Wmk inverted and reversed		50·00	30·00
61	9d. olive-green (R.)		3·00	5·50
	a. No accent		£250	£275
62	10d. turquoise-blue		16·00	48·00
63	1s. bistre-brown		7·00	10·00
	a. No accent		£5500	£6500
	b. Accent inserted by hand		£600	£650
64	2s. 6d. chocolate-brown		35·00	55·00
	a. Major Re-entry		£850	£950
	b. No accent		£350	£400
	c. Accent reversed		£425	£475

65	5s. rose-red		65·00	£120
	a. No accent		£450	£500
	b. Accent reversed		£550	£600
66	10s. dull grey-blue		£140	£275
	a. No accent		£2000	£2500
	b. Accent reversed		£2750	£3500
52/66		Set of 15	£250	£500

The accents inserted by hand are in dull black. The reversed accents are grave (thus "à") instead of acute ("á"). A variety with "S" of "Saorstat" directly over "é" of "éireann", instead of to left, may be found in all values except the 2½d. and 4d. In the 2s. 6d., 5s. and 10s. it is very slightly to the left in the "S" over "é" variety, bringing the "á" of "Saorstat" directly above the last "n" of "éireann".

(*b*) *Optd with T 5, in dull or shiny blue-black, by Harrison, for use in horiz or vert coils* (7.3.23)
67	½d. green		1·75	9·50
	a. Long "1" in "1922"		20·00	48·00
	y. Wmk inverted and reversed			
68	1d. scarlet		4·00	9·50
	a. Long "1" in "1922"		75·00	£140
69	1½d. red-brown		6·00	40·00
	a. Long "1" in "1922"		85·00	£225
70	2d. orange (Die II)		6·00	8·50
	a. Long "I" in "1922"		26·00	45·00
	w. Wmk inverted		—	£150
67/70		Set of 4	16·00	60·00

In the Harrison overprint the characters are rather bolder than those of the Thom overprint, and the foot of the "1" of "1922" is usually rounded instead of square. The long "1" in "1922" has a serif at foot. The second "e" of "éireann" appears to be slightly raised.

PRINTERS. The following and all subsequent issues to No. 148 were printed at the Government Printing Works, Dublin, *unless otherwise stated.*

6 "Sword of Light"　7 Map of Ireland　8 Arms of Ireland

9 Celtic Cross　　10

(Des J. J. O'Reilly, T 6; J. Ingram, T 7; Miss M. Girling, T 8; and Miss L. Williams, T 9. Typo. Plates made by Royal Mint, London)

1922 (6 Dec)–**34.** W **10.** *P* 15×14.
71	6	½d. bright green (20.4.23)	85	75
		a. Imperf × perf 14, wmk sideways (11.34)	24·00	45·00
		w. Wmk inverted	30·00	15·00
72	7	1d. carmine (23.2.23)	90	10
		a. Perf 15 × imperf (single perf) (1933)	85·00	£160
		c. Perf 15 × imperf (7.34)	18·00	40·00
		cw. Wmk inverted		
		d. Booklet pane. Three stamps plus three printed labels (21.8.31)	£225	
		dw. Wmk inverted		
73		1½d. claret (2.2.23)	1·40	1·75
		w. Wmk inverted		
74		2d. grey-green (6.12.22)	1·25	10
		a. Imperf × perf 14, wmk sideways (11.34)	42·00	70·00
		b. Perf 15 × imperf (1934)	£8500	£1500
		w. Wmk inverted	20·00	5·00
		y. Wmk inverted and reversed	30·00	7·00

75	8	2¹/₂d. red-brown (7.9.23) ..	..	..	3·75	3·50
		w. Wmk inverted	..	..	50·00	8·00
76	9	3d. ultramarine (16.3.23)		..	1·75	75
		w. Wmk inverted	..	..	65·00	12·00
77	8	4d. slate-blue (28.9.23)		..	2·00	3·25
		w. Wmk inverted	..	..	75·00	25·00
78	6	5d. deep violet (11.5.23)		..	8·00	9·50
		w. Wmk inverted	..	..		
79		6d. claret (21.12.23)	..	..	3·75	3·50
		w. Wmk inverted	..	..	£110	25·00
80	8	9d. deep violet (26.10.23)		..	13·00	9·00
		w. Wmk inverted	..	..		
81	9	10d. brown (11.5.23)	..	..	9·00	18·00
82	6	1s. light blue (15.6.23)		..	17·00	5·50
		w. Wmk inverted	..			
71/82				*Set of* 12	55·00	50·00

No. 72a is imperf vertically except for a single perf at each top corner. It was issued for use in automatic machines.
See also Nos. 111/22 and 227/8.

Saorstát
éireann
1922

(11 Narrow Date)   12 Daniel O'Connell

1925 (Aug)–**28**. *Stamps of Great Britain (Bradbury, Wilkinson printing) optd at the Government Printing Works, Dublin or by Harrison and Sons. (a) With T* 11 *in black or grey-black* (25.8.25).

83	2s. 6d. chocolate-brown		..	38·00	80·00
	a. Wide and narrow date (pair) (1927)			£250	
84	5s. rose-red	..	..	50·00	£120
	a. Wide and narrow date (pair) (1927)			£400	
85	10s. dull grey-blue	..	..	£110	£275
	a. Wide and narrow date (pair) (1927)			£1000	
83/5	..	..	*Set of* 3	£180	£425

The varieties with wide and narrow date *se-tenant* are from what is known as the "composite setting," in which some stamps showed the wide date, as T 5, while in others the figures were close together, as in T 11.
Single specimens of this printing with wide date may be distinguished from Nos. 64 to 66 by the colour of the ink, which is black or grey-black in the composite setting and blue-black in the Thom printing.
The type of the "composite" overprint usually shows distinct signs of wear.

(b) *As T* 5 (*wide date*) *in black* (1927–28)

86	2s. 6d. chocolate-brown (9.12.27)		..	42·00	42·00
	a. Circumflex accent over "a"		..	£200	£250
	b. No accent over "a"		..	£350	£375
	c. Flat accent on "a"		..	£300	£350
87	5s. rose-red (2.28)		..	60·00	80·00
	a. Circumflex accent over "a"		..	£325	£375
	c. Flat accent on "a"		..	£400	£450
88	10s. dull grey-blue (15.2.28)		..	£150	£170
	a. Circumflex accent over "a"		..	£800	£900
	c. Flat accent on "a"		..	£900	£1000
86/8	..	..	*Set of* 3	£225	£250

This printing can be distinguished from the Thom overprints in dull black, by the clear, heavy impression (in deep black) which often shows in relief on the back of the stamp.
The variety showing a circumflex accent over the "a" occurred on R.9/2. The overprint in this position finally deteriorated to such an extent that some examples of the 2s. 6d. were without accent (No. 86b). A new cliché was then introduced with the accent virtually flat and which also showed damage to the "a" and the crossbar of the "t".

(Des L. Whelan. Typo)

1929 (22 June). *Catholic Emancipation Centenary.* W10. *P* 15 × 14.

89	12	2d. grey-green ..		..	50	45
90		3d. blue ..	..	..	4·00	8·50
91		9d. bright violet		..	4·00	4·00
89/91 ..		..	..	*Set of* 3	7·50	11·50

13 Shannon Barrage   14 Reaper

(Des E. L. Lawrenson. Typo)

1930 (15 Oct). *Completion of Shannon Hydro-Electric Scheme.* W 10. *P* 15 × 14.

92	13	2d. agate	..	..	80	55

(T **14** and **15** des G. Atkinson. Typo)

1931 (12 June). *Bicentenary of the Royal Dublin Society.* W 10. *P* 15 × 14.

93	14	2d. blue ..	..	..	65	30

15 The Cross of   16 Adoration of the   17 Hurler.
Cong   Cross

1932 (12 May). *International Eucharistic Congress.* W 10. *P* 15×14.

94	15	2d. grey-green ..		..	90	30
		w. Wmk inverted	..	..		
95		3d. blue ..	..	..	2·25	5·00

(T **16** to **19** des R. J. King. Typo)

1933 (18 Sept). *"Holy Year".* W 10. *P* 15 × 14.

96	16	2d. grey-green ..		..	1·00	15
97		3d. blue ..	..	..	2·50	2·00

1934 (27 July). *Golden Jubilee of the Gaelic Athletic Association.* W 10. *P* 15 × 14.

98	17	2d. green	..	..	75	45

1935 (Mar–July). *Stamps of Great Britain (Waterlow printings) optd as T* 5 (*wide date*), *at the Government Printing Works, Dublin.*

99	2s. 6d. chocolate (No. 450)		..	45·00	48·00
	a. Flat accent on "a" (R. 9/2)		..	£225	£200
100	5s. bright rose-red (No. 451)		..	80·00	80·00
	a. Flat accent on "a" (R. 9/2)		..	£300	£250
101	10s. indigo (No. 452)		..	£350	£350
	a. Flat accent on "a" (R. 9/2)		..	£900	£750
99/101	..		*Set of* 3	£425	£425

On Nos. 99/101 the background around King George V's portrait consists of both horizontal and diagonal lines. All earlier overprints show a background of horizontal lines only.

18 St. Patrick   19 Ireland and New Constitution

1937 (8 Sept). W 10. *P* 14×15.

102	18	2s. 6d. emerald-green ..		..	£140	65·00
		w. Wmk inverted	..	..	£600	£225
103		5s. maroon	..	..	£180	£110
		w. Wmk inverted	..	..	£500	£225

104	18	10s. deep blue			£140	50·00
		w. Wmk inverted				
102/4				*Set of* 3	£425	£200

See also Nos. 123/5.

EIRE

29 December 1937—17 April 1949

1937 (29 Dec). *Constitution Day.* W **10**. P 15×14.

105	**19**	2d. claret			1·00	20
		w. Wmk inverted			—	£180
106		3d. blue			4·00	3·50

For similar stamps see Nos. 176/7.

20 Father Mathew

(Des S. Keating. Typo)

1938 (1 July). *Centenary of Temperance Crusade.* W **10**. P 15×14.

107	**20**	2d. black			1·50	30
		w. Wmk inverted				
108		3d. blue			8·50	6·00

21 George Washington, American Eagle and Irish Harp

22

(Des G. Atkinson. Typo)

1939 (1 Mar). *150th Anniv of U.S. Constitution and Installation of First U.S. President.* W **10**. P 15 × 14.

109	**21**	2d. scarlet			1·75	60
110		3d. blue			3·25	4·00

SIZE OF WATERMARK. T **22** can be found in various sizes from about 8 to 10 mm high. This is due to the use of two different dandy rolls supplied by different firms and to the effects of paper shrinkage and other factors such as pressure and machine speed.

White line above left value tablet joining horizontal line to ornament (R. 3/7)

1940–68. Typo. W **22**. P 15×14 *or* 14×15 (2s. 6d. *to* 10s.).

111	**6**	½d. bright green (24.11.40)			2·00	40
		w. Wmk inverted			50·00	6·50
112	**7**	1d. carmine (26.10.40)			30	10
		aw. Wmk inverted			1·60	25
		b. From coils. Perf 14×imperf (9.40)			65·00	65·00
		c. From coils. Perf 15×imperf (20.3.46)			40·00	15·00
		cw. Wmk inverted			40·00	15·00
		d. Booklet pane. Three stamps plus three printed labels			£1500	
		dw. Wmk inverted				

113	**7**	1½d. claret (1.40)			13·00	30
		w. Wmk inverted			29·00	7·50
114		2d. grey-green (1.40)			30	10
		w. Wmk inverted			2·25	75
115	**8**	2½d. red-brown (3.41)			9·00	15
		w. Wmk inverted			19·00	4·00
116	**9**	3d. blue (12.40)			60	10
		w. Wmk inverted			3·50	50
117	**8**	4d. slate-blue (12.40)			55	10
		w. Wmk inverted			13·00	2·75
118	**6**	5d. deep violet (7.40)			65	10
		w. Wmk inverted			26·00	1·50
119		6d. claret (3.42)			2·25	50
		aw. Wmk inverted			18·00	3·00
		b. Chalk-surfaced paper (1967)			1·25	20
		bw. Wmk inverted			13·00	2·50
119c		8d. scarlet (12.9.49)			80	70
		cw. Wmk inverted			32·00	10·00
120	**8**	9d. deep violet (7.40)			1·50	70
		w. Wmk inverted			9·50	2·00
121	**9**	10d. brown (7.40)			60	70
		aw. Wmk inverted			10·00	3·50
121b		11d. rose (12.9.49)			1·50	2·25
122	**6**	1s. light blue (6.40)			80·00	17·00
		w. Wmk inverted			£600	£150
123	**18**	2s. 6d. emerald-green (10.2.43)			40·00	1·25
		aw. Wmk inverted			80·00	20·00
		b. Chalk-surfaced paper (1968?)			1·50	2·25
		bw. Wmk inverted			28·00	4·00
124		5s. maroon (15.12.42)			40·00	3·00
		a. Line flaw				
		bw. Wmk inverted			£150	30·00
		c. Chalk-surfaced paper (1968?)			13·00	4·00
		ca. Purple			6·00	7·50
		cb. Line flaw			80·00	
		cw. Wmk inverted			35·00	9·00
125		10s. deep blue (7.45)			60·00	6·00
		aw. Wmk inverted			£170	65·00
		b. Chalk-surfaced paper (1968)			19·00	11·00
		ba. Blue			9·00	16·00
		bw. Wmk inverted			£120	55·00
111/25				*Set of* 17	£110	30·00

There is a wide range of shades and also variation in paper used in this issue.

See also Nos. 227/8.

1941 **J ᴄᴜɪ́ᵐ̇ɴᴇ ᴀɪꙅᴇ́ɪʀᴅ̇ᴇ 1916**

(*23 Trans* "In memory of the rising of 1916")

24 Volunteer and G.P.O., Dublin

1941 (12 Apr). *25th Anniv of Easter Rising* (1916). *Provisional issue.* T **7** and **9** (2d. *in new colour*), optd *with* T **23**.

126	**7**	2d. orange (G.)			1·50	50
127	**9**	3d. blue (V.)			27·00	9·50

(Des V. Brown. Typo)

1941 (27 Oct). *25th Anniv of Easter Rising* (1916). *Definitive issue.* W **22**. P 15 × 14.

128	**24**	2½d. blue-black			70	60

25 Dr. Douglas Hyde

26 Sir William Rowan Hamilton

27 Bro. Michael O'Clery

(Des S. O'Sullivan. Typo)

1943 (31 July). *50th Anniv of Founding of Gaelic League.* W **22**. P 15 × 14.

129	**25**	½d. green			40	30
130		2½d. claret			1·25	10

(Des S. O'Sullivan from a bust by Hogan. Typo)

1943 (13 Nov). *Centenary of Announcement of Discovery of Quaternions.* W **22**. P 15 × 14.

131	**26**	¹/₂d. green	..	..	..	..	40	40
		w. Wmk inverted	..	..	..		
132		2¹/₂d. brown	..	..	..	..	1·75	10

(Des R. J. King. Typo)

1944 (30 June). *Tercentenary of Death of Michael O'Clery. (Commemorating the "Annals of the Four Masters").* W **22** *(sideways*).* P 14×15.

133	**27**	¹/₂d. emerald-green	..	..	..	10	10
		w. Wmk facing right	..	..	55	20
134		1s. red-brown	..	..	..	70	10
		w. Wmk facing right	..	..	2·25	50

*The normal sideways watermark shows the top of the e facing left, *as seen from the back of the stamp.*

Although issued as commemoratives these two stamps were kept in use as part of the current issue, replacing Nos. 111 and 122.

28 Edmund Ignatius Rice   29 "Youth Sowing Seeds of Freedom"

(Des S. O'Sullivan. Typo)

1944 (29 Aug). *Death Centenary of Edmund Rice (founder of Irish Christian Brothers).* W **22**. P 15 × 14.

135	**28**	2¹/₂d. slate	..	..	..	60	45
		w. Wmk inverted	..	..		

(Des R. J. King. Typo)

1945 (15 Sept). *Centenary of Death of Thomas Davis (founder of Young Ireland Movement).* W **22**. P 15 × 14.

136	**29**	2¹/₂d. blue	..	..	..	1·00	25
		w. Wmk inverted	..	..	—	£130
137		6d. claret	..	..	..	7·00	3·75

30 "Country and Homestead"

(Des R. J. King. Typo)

1946 (16 Sept). *Birth Centenaries of Davitt and Parnell (land reformers).* W **22**. P 15 × 14.

138	**30**	2¹/₂d. scarlet	..	..	..	1·50	15
139		3d. blue	..	..	..	3·50	3·50

31 Angel Victor over Rock of Cashel

(Des R. J. King. Recess Waterlow (1d. to 1s. 3d. until 1961), D.L.R. (8d., 1s. 3d. from 1961 and 1s. 5d.))

1948 (7 Apr)–**65**. *Air. T* **31** *and similar horiz designs.* W **22**. P 15 (1s. 5d.) *or* 15 × 14 *(others).*

140	**31**	1d. chocolate (4.4.49)	..	..	2·00	3·50
141	–	3d. blue	..	..	..	4·00	2·25

142	–	6d. magenta	..	..	..	1·00	1·50
		aw. Wmk inverted	..	..		
142b	–	8d. lake-brown (13.12.54)	..	7·00	7·00
143	–	1s. green (4.4.49)	..	..	1·25	1·50
143a	**31**	1s. 3d. red-orange (13.12.54)	..	7·50	1·25
		aw. Wmk inverted	..	..	£550	£250
143b		1s. 5d. deep ultramarine (1.4.65)	..	3·50	1·00
140/3b			..		*Set of* 7	24·00	16·00

Designs:—3d., 8d. Lough Derg; 6d. Croagh Patrick; 1s. Glendalough.

35 Theobald Wolfe Tone

(Des K. Uhlemann. Typo)

1948 (19 Nov). *150th Anniv of Insurrection.* W **22**. P 15×14.

144	**35**	2¹/₂d. reddish purple	..	..	1·00	10
		w. Wmk inverted	..	..		
145		3d. violet	..	..	..	3·25	3·25

REPUBLIC OF IRELAND

18 April 1949

36 Leinster House and Arms of Provinces   37 J. C. Mangan

(Des Muriel Brandt. Typo)

1949 (21 Nov). *International Recognition of Republic.* W **22**. P 15 × 14.

146	**36**	2¹/₂d. reddish brown	..	..	1·50	10
147		3d. bright blue	..	..	..	5·50	4·00

(Des R. J. King. Typo)

1949 (5 Dec). *Death Centenary of James Clarence Mangan (poet).* W **22**. P 15 × 14.

148	**37**	1d. green	..	..	..	1·50	20
		w. Wmk inverted	..	..		

38 Statue of St. Peter, Rome   39 Thomas Moore   40 Irish Harp

(Recess Waterlow & Sons)

1950 (11 Sept). *Holy Year.* W **22**. P 12¹/₂.

149	**38**	2¹/₂d. violet	..	..	..	1·00	40
150		3d. blue	..	..	..	8·00	8·50
151		9d. brown	..	..	..	8·00	10·00
149/51			..	..		*Set of* 3	15·00	17·00

PRINTERS. Nos. 152 to 200 were recess-printed by De La Rue & Co, Dublin, *unless otherwise stated.*

(Eng W. Vacek)

1952 (10 Nov). *Death Centenary of Thomas Moore (poet). W* **22.** *P* 13.

152	**39**	2½d. reddish purple	..	..	50	10
153		3½d. deep olive-green	..	..	1·75	2·75

(Des F. O'Ryan. Typo Government Printing Works, Dublin)

1953 (9 Feb). *"An Tostal" (Ireland at Home) Festival. W* **22** *(sideways). P* 14 × 15.

154	**40**	2½d. emerald-green	..	..	1·25	35
155		1s. 4d. blue	..	..	15·00	24·00

41 Robert Emmet

42 Madonna and Child (Della Robbia)

43 Cardinal Newman (first Rector)

(Eng L. Downey)

1953 (21 Sept). *150th Death Anniv of Emmet (patriot). W* **22.** *P* 13.

156	**41**	3d. deep bluish green	..	..	3·75	15
157		1s. 3d. carmine..	..	..	42·00	9·50

(Eng A. R. Lane)

1954 (24 May). *Marian Year. W* **22.** *P* 15.

158	**42**	3d. blue ..	..	..	1·50	10
159		5d. myrtle-green	..	..	2·75	5·50

(Des L. Whelan. Typo Govt Printing Works, Dublin)

1954 (19 July). *Centenary of Founding of Catholic University of Ireland. W* **22.** *P* 15 × 14.

160	**43**	2d. bright purple	..	..	1·50	10
		w. Wmk inverted	..	..	—	£180
161		1s. 3d. blue	..	..	16·00	6·00

44 Statue of Commodore Barry

45 John Redmond

46 Thomas O'Crohan

(Des and eng H. Woyty-Wimmer)

1956 (16 Sept). *Barry Commemoration. W* **22.** *P* 15.

162	**44**	3d. slate-lilac	..	..	2·00	10
163		1s. 3d. deep blue	..	..	7·00	9·00

1957 (11 June). *Birth Centenary of John Redmond (politician). W* **22.** *P* 15 × 14.

164	**45**	3d. deep blue	..	..	1·25	10
165		1s. 3d. brown-purple	..	..	10·00	15·00

1957 (1 July). *Birth Centenary of Thomas O'Crohan (author). W* **22.** *P* 14 × 15.

166	**46**	2d. maroon	..	..	1·50	15
		a. Wmk sideways	..	..	†	—
167		5d. violet	..	..	1·50	5·50

47 Admiral Brown

48 "Father Wadding" (Ribera)

49 Tom Clarke

(Des S. O'Sullivan. Typo Govt Printing Works, Dublin)

1957 (23 Sept). *Death Centenary of Admiral William Brown. W* **22.** *P* 15 × 14.

168	**47**	3d. blue ..	..	..	2·25	20
169		1s. 3d. carmine..	..	..	30·00	16·00

1957 (25 Nov). *300th Death Anniv of Father Luke Wadding (theologian). W* **22.** *P* 15.

170	**48**	3d. deep blue	..	..	2·00	10
171		1s. 3d. lake	..	..	17·00	8·50

1958 (28 July). *Birth Centenary of Thomas J. ("Tom") Clarke (patriot). W* **22.** *P* 15.

172	**49**	3d. deep green ..	..	..	2·50	10
173		1s. 3d. red-brown	..	..	6·50	13·00

50 Mother Mary Aikenhead

51 Arthur Guinness

(Eng Waterlow. Recess Imprimerie Belge de Securité, Brussels subsidiary of Waterlow & Sons)

1958 (20 Oct). *Death Centenary of Mother Mary Aikenhead (foundress of Irish Sisters of Charity). W* **22.** *P* 15 × 14.

174	**50**	3d. Prussian blue	..	..	1·75	10
175		1s. 3d. rose-carmine	..	..	15·00	10·00

(Typo Govt Printing Works, Dublin)

1958 (29 Dec). *21st Anniv of the Irish Constitution. W* **22.** *P* 15 × 14.

176	**19**	3d. brown	..	..	1·25	10
177		5d. emerald-green	..	..	2·25	4·50

1959 (20 July). *Bicentenary of Guinness Brewery. W* **22.** *P* 15.

178	**51**	3d. brown-purple	..	..	4·00	10
179		1s. 3d. blue	..	..	14·00	12·00

52 "The Flight of the Holy Family"

(Des K. Uhlemann)

1960 (20 June). *World Refugee Year. W* **22.** *P* 15.

180	**52**	3d. purple	..	..	50	10
181		1s. 3d. sepia	..	..	75	3·25

53 Conference Emblem

(Des P. Rahikainen)

1960 (19 Sept). *Europa. W 22. P* 15.
182   **53**   6d. light brown ..   ..   4·00   3·00
183   1s. 3d. violet   ..   ..   ..   10·00   20·00
   The ink of No. 183 is fugitive.

54 Dublin Airport, De   **55** St. Patrick
Havilland D.H.84 Dragon
Mk 2 *Iolar* and Boeing 720

(Des J. Flanagan and D. R. Lowther)

1961 (26 June). *25th Anniv of Aer Lingus. W 22. P* 15.
184   **54**   6d. blue   ..   ..   ..   1·00   3·25
         w. Wmk inverted   ..   ..   ..
185   1s. 3d. green   ..   ..   ..   1·50   4·75

(Recess B.W.)

1961 (25 Sept). *Fifteenth Death Centenary of St. Patrick. W 22. P* 14½.
186   **55**   3d. blue ..   ..   1·25   10
187   8d. purple   ..   ..   ..   2·25   5·50
188   1s. 3d. green   ..   ..   2·50   1·60
186/8 ..   ..   *Set of* 3   5·50   6·50

56 John O'Donovan and
Eugene O'Curry

(Recess B.W.)

1962 (26 Mar). *Death Centenaries of O'Donovan and O'Curry (scholars). W 22. P* 15.
189   **56**   3d. carmine   40   10
190   1s. 3d. purple   ..   ..   ..   1·50   2·50

57 Europa "Tree"

(Des L. Weyer)

1962 (17 Sept). *Europa. W 22. P* 15.
191   **57**   6d. carmine-red   50   1·00
192   1s. 3d. turquoise   90   1·50

58 Campaign Emblem

(Des K. Uhlemann)

1963 (21 Mar). *Freedom from Hunger. W 22. P* 15.
193   **58**   4d. deep violet   50   10
194   1s. 3d. scarlet   ..   ..   ..   1·75   2·75

59 "Co-operation"

(Des A. Holm)

1963 (16 Sept). *Europa. W 22. P* 15.
195   **59**   6d. carmine   75   75
196   1s. 3d. blue   ..   ..   ..   2·00   3·75

60 Centenary Emblem

(Des P. Wildbur. Photo Harrison & Sons)

1963 (2 Dec). *Centenary of Red Cross. W 22. P* 14½ × 14.
197   **60**   4d. red and grey   50   10
198   1s. 3d. red, grey and light emerald   ..   1·25   2·25

61 Wolfe Tone

(Des P. Wildbur)

1964 (13 Apr). *Birth Bicentenary of Wolfe Tone (revolutionary). W 22. P* 15.
199   **61**   4d. black   75   10
200   1s. 3d. ultramarine   ..   ..   2·25   2·25

62 Irish Pavilion at Fair

(Des A. Devane. Photo Harrison & Sons)

1964 (20 July). *New York World's Fair. W 22. P* 14½ × 14.
201   **62**   5d. blue-grey, brown, violet & yellow-ol   50   10
         a. Brown omitted* £1200
202   5d. blue-grey, brown, turquoise-blue
         and light yellow-green   ..   2·25   3·75
   *No. 201a comes from the top row of a sheet and shows part of the brown cross which would appear in the sheet margin. As the second horizontal row was normal it would appear that the brown cylinder was incorrectly registered.

63 Europa "Flower"   **64** "Waves of Communication"

(Des G. Bétemps. Photo Harrison)

1964 (14 Sept). *Europa. W* **22** (*sideways*). *P* 14 × 14½.
203   **63**   8d. olive-green and blue   1·25   1·25
204   1s. 5d. red-brown and orange   ..   3·25   2·75

(Des P. Wildbur. Photo Harrison)

1965 (17 May). *I.T.U. Centenary. W* **22**. *P* 14½ × 14.
205   **64**   3d. blue and green   40   10
206   8d. black and green   ..   ..   1·10   2·00

PRINTERS. Nos. 207 onwards were photogravure-printed by the Stamping Branch of the Revenue Commissioners, Dublin *unless otherwise stated.*

65 W. B. Yeats (poet)   **66** I.C.Y. Emblem

(Des R. Kyne, from drawing by S. O'Sullivan)

1965 (14 June). *Yeats' Birth Centenary. W* **22** (*sideways*). *P* 15.
207   **65**   5d. black, orange-brown and deep green   30   10
208   1s. 5d. black, grey-green and brown   ..   2·25   1·75

1965 (16 Aug). *International Co-operation Year. W* **22**. *P* 15.
209   **66**   3d. ultramarine and new blue   60   10
210   10d. deep brown and brown   ..   ..   1·00   3·00

67 Europa "Sprig"

(Des H. Karlsson)

1965 (27 Sept). *Europa. W* **22**. *P* 15.
211   **67**   8d. black and brown-red   ..   ..   1·00   1·00
212   1s. 5d. purple and light turquoise-blue   3·00   3·50

68 James Connolly

69 "Marching to Freedom"

(Des E. Delaney (No. 216), R. Kyne, after portraits by S. O'Sullivan (others))

1966 (12 Apr). *50th Anniv of Easter Rising. T* **68/9** *and similar horiz portraits. W* **22**. *P* 15.
213   3d. black and greenish blue   35   10
      a. Horiz pair. Nos. 213/14   70   2·50
214   3d. black and bronze-green   35   10
215   5d. black and yellow-olive   35   10
      a. Horiz pair. Nos. 215/16   70   2·50
216   5d. black, orange and blue-green   35   10
217   7d. black and light orange-brown   40   2·25
      a. Horiz pair. Nos. 217/18   80   7·50
218   7d. black and blue-green   40   2·25
219   1s. 5d. black and turquoise   40   1·50
      a. Horiz pair. Nos. 219/20   80   9·00
220   1s. 5d. black and bright green   40   1·50
213/20   ..   ..   ..   *Set of* 8   2·75   7·00
Designs:—No. 213, Type **68**; No. 214, Thomas J. Clarke; No. 215, P. H. Pearse; No. 216, Type **69**; No. 217, Eamonn Ceannt; No. 218, Sean MacDiarmada; No. 219, Thomas MacDonagh; No. 220, Joseph Plunkett.
Nos. 213/14, 215/16, 217/18 and 219/20 were each printed together, *se-tenant*, in horizontal pairs throughout the sheet.

76 R. Casement   **77** Europa "Ship"

(Des R. Kyne)

1966 (3 Aug). *50th Death Anniv of Roger Casement (patriot). W* **22** (*sideways*). *P* 15.
221   **76**   5d. black   15   10
222   1s. red-brown   30   50

(Des R. Kyne, after G. and J. Bender)

1966 (26 Sept). *Europa. W* **22** (*sideways*). *P* 15.
223   **77**   7d. emerald and orange   35   40
224   1s. 5d. emerald and light grey..   ..   90   1·00

78 Interior of Abbey (from lithograph)   **79** Cogwheels

1966 (8 Nov). *750th Anniv of Ballintubber Abbey. W* **22**. *P* 15.
225   **78**   5d. red-brown   10   10
226   1s. black   20   25

1966–67. As Nos. 116, 118 but photo. Smaller design (17×21 mm). Chalk-surfaced paper. W **22**. P 15.

227	9	3d. blue (1.8.67)	..	..	40	15
228	6	5d. bright violet (1.12.66)	..	..	30	15
		w. Wmk inverted (from booklets)	..	1·75	1·25

No. 228 was only issued in booklets at first but was released in sheets on 1.4.68 in a slightly brighter shade. In the sheet stamps the lines of shading are more regular.

(Des O. Bonnevalle)

1967 (2 May). Europa. W **22** (sideways). P 15.

229	79	7d. light emerald, gold and pale cream	30	40
230		1s. 5d. carmine-red, gold and pale cream	70	1·00

80 Maple Leaves

(Des P. Hickey)

1967 (28 Aug). Canadian Centennial. W **22**. P 15.

231	80	5d. multicoloured	..	..	10	10
232		1s. 5d. multicoloured	..	..	20	60

81 Rock of Cashel (from photo by Edwin Smith)

1967 (25 Sept). International Tourist Year. W **22** (inverted). P 15.

233	81	7d. sepia	..	..	..	15	20
234		10d. slate-blue	..	..	..	15	40

82 1 c. Fenian Stamp Essay	83 24 c. Fenian Stamp Essay

1967 (23 Oct). Centenary of Fenian Rising. W **22** (sideways). P 15.

235	82	5d. black and light green	..	..	10	10
236	83	1s. black and light pink	..	..	20	30

84 Jonathan Swift	85 Gulliver and Lilliputians

(Des M. Byrne)

1967 (30 Nov). 300th Birth Anniv of Jonathan Swift. W **22** (sideways). P 15.

237	84	3d. black and olive-grey	..	..	10	10
238	85	1s. 5d. blackish brown and pale blue	..	20	20

86 Europa "Key"

(Des H. Schwarzenbach and M. Biggs)

1968 (29 Apr). Europa. W **22**. P 15.

239	86	7d. brown-red, gold and brown	..	..	25	50
240		1s. 5d. new blue, gold and brown	..	40	1·00

87 St Mary's Cathedral, Limerick

(Des from photo by J. J. Bambury. Recess B.W.)

1968 (26 Aug). 800th Anniv of St. Mary's Cathedral, Limerick. W **22**. P 15.

241	87	5d. Prussian blue	..	..	..	10	10
242		10d. yellow-green	..	..	..	20	60

88 Countess Markievicz	89 James Connolly

1968 (23 Sept). Birth Centenary of Countess Markievicz (patriot). W **22**. P 15.

243	88	3d. black	..	..	..	10	10
244		1s. 5d. deep blue and blue	..	..	20	20

1968 (23 Sept). Birth Centenary of James Connolly (patriot). W **22** (sideways). P 15.

245	89	6d. deep brown and chocolate	..	..	15	50
246		1s. blksh grn, apple-grn & myrtle-grn	15	10

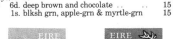

90 Stylised Dog (brooch)	91 Stag

92 Winged Ox (Symbol of St. Luke)

93 Eagle (Symbol of St. John The Evangelist)

(Des H. Gerl)

1968–70. *Pence values expressed with "p". W 22 (sideways* on ½d. to 1s. 9d.). P 15.*

247	**90**	½d. red-orange (7.6.69)	..	10	30
248		1d. pale yellow-green (7.6.69)	..	15	10
		a. Coil stamp. Perf 14×15 (8.70?)	..	90	3·00
249		2d. light ochre (14.10.68)	..	50	10
		a. Coil stamp. Perf 14×15 (8.70?)	..	90	3·75
250		3d. blue (7.6.69)	..	35	10
		a. Coil stamp. Perf 14×15 (8.70?)	..	90	3·75
251		4d. deep brown-red (31.3.69)	..	30	10
252		5d. myrtle-green (31.3.69)	..	40	35
253		6d. bistre-brown (24.2.69)	..	30	10
		w. Wmk e facing right	..	5·50	1·50
254	**91**	7d. brown and yellow (7.6.69)	..	45	3·50
255		8d. chocolate & orge-brown (14.10.68)	..	45	1·00
256		9d. slate-blue and olive-green (24.2.69)	..	50	10
257		10d. chocolate and bluish violet (31.3.69)		1·50	1·50
258		1s. chocolate and red-brown (31.3.69)		40	10
259		1s. 9d. black & lt turquoise-bl (24.2.69)		4·00	1·50
260	**92**	2s. 6d. multicoloured (14.10.68)	..	1·75	30
261		5s. multicoloured (24.2.69)	..	3·00	10
262	**93**	10s. multicoloured (14.10.68)	..	4·50	3·75
247/62		..	*Set of* 16	16·00	12·50

*The normal sideways watermark shows the top of the e facing left, *as seen from the back of the stamp.*

The 1d., 2d., 3d., 5d., 6d., 9d., 1s. and 2s. 6d. exist with PVA gum as well as gum arabic. The coil stamps exist on PVA only, and the rest on gum arabic only.

See also Nos. 287/301, 339/59 and 478/83.

94 Human Rights Emblem

95 Dail Eireann Assembly

1968 (4 Nov). *Human Rights Year. W 22 (sideways). P 15.*

263	**94**	5d. yellow, gold and black	.. ..	15	10
264		7d. yellow, gold and red	.. ..	15	40

(Des M. Byrne)

1969 (21 Jan). *50th Anniv of Dail Eireann (First National Parliament). W 22 (sideways). P 15 × 14½.*

265	**95**	6d. myrtle-green	.. ..	15	10
266		9d. Prussian blue	.. ..	15	30

96 Colonnade

97 Quadruple I.L.O. Emblems

(Des L. Gasbarra and G. Belli; adapted Myra Maguire)

1969 (28 Apr). *Europa. W 22. P 15.*

267	**96**	9d. grey, ochre and ultramarine	..	40	1·10
268		1s. 9d. grey, gold and scarlet	..	70	1·40

(Des K. C. Däbczewski)

1969 (14 July). *50th Anniv of International Labour Organization. W 22 (sideways). P 15.*

269	**97**	6d. black and grey	.. ..	20	10
270		9d. black and yellow	.. ..	20	25

98 "The Last Supper and Crucifixion" (Evie Hone Window, Eton Chapel)

(Des R. Kyne)

1969 (1 Sept). *Contemporary Irish Art (1st issue). W 22 (sideways). P 15 × 14½.*

271	**98**	1s. multicoloured	..	30	1·50

See also Nos. 280, 306, 317, 329, 362, 375, 398, 408, 452, 470 and 498.

99 Mahatma Gandhi

1969 (2 Oct). *Birth Centenary of Mahatma Gandhi. W 22. P 15.*

272	**99**	6d. black and green	.. ..	20	10
273		1s. 9d. black and yellow	..	30	90

100 Symbolic Bird in Tree

(Des D. Harrington)

1970 (23 Feb). *European Conservation Year. W 22. P 15.*

274	**100**	6d. bistre and black	.. ..	20	10
275		9d. slate-violet and black	..	25	80

101 "Flaming Sun"

(Des L. le Brocquy)

1970 (4 May). *Europa.* W **22**. *P* 15.
276	**101**	6d. bright violet and silver		30	10
277		9d. brown and silver	..	45	1·25
278		1s. 9d. deep olive-grey and silver	..	65	2·00
276/8	..	.. .. ..	*Set of 3*	1·25	3·00

102 "Sailing Boats"
(Peter Monamy)

103 "Madonna of
Eire" (Mainie Jellett)

(Des P. Wildbur and P. Scott)

1970 (13 July). *250th Anniv of Royal Cork Yacht Club.* W **22**.
P 15.
279	**102**	4d. multicoloured	.. .. ..	15	10

1970 (1 Sept). *Contemporary Irish Art (2nd issue).* W **22** *(sideways).* P 15.
280	**103**	1s. multicoloured	.. .. ..	15	20

104 Thomas
MacCurtain

106 Kevin Barry

(Des P. Wildbur)

1970 (26 Oct). *50th Death Anniversaries of Irish Patriots.* T **104**
and similar vert design. W **22** *(sideways).* P 15.
281	9d. black, bluish violet and greyish black	..	50	25
	a. Pair. Nos. 281/2	.. ..	1·00	2·50
282	9d. black, bluish violet and greyish black		50	25
283	2s. 9d. black, new blue and greyish black	..	1·75	1·50
	a. Pair. Nos. 283/4	.. ..	3·75	11·00
284	2s. 9d. black, new blue and greyish black	..	1·75	1·50
281/4	.. ..	*Set of 4*	4·50	3·25

Designs:—Nos. 281 and 283, Type **104**; others, Terence
MacSwiney.
Nos. 281/2 and 283/4 were each printed together, *se-tenant*, in
horizontal and vertical pairs throughout the sheet.

(Des P. Wildbur)

1970 (2 Nov). *50th Death Anniv of Kevin Barry (patriot).* W **22**
(inverted). P 15.
285	**106**	6d. olive-green	.. .. ..	40	10
286		1s. 2d. royal blue	.. ..	55	1·40

106a Stylized Dog
(Brooch)

107 "Europa Chain"

Two types of 10 p.:
I. Outline and markings of the ox in lilac.
II. Outline and markings in brown.

1971 (15 Feb)–**75**. *Decimal Currency. Designs as Nos. 247/62
but with "p" omitted as in T* **106a**. *W* **22** *(sideways* on 10, 12,
20 and 50p.). P 15.*
287	**106a**	½p. bright green	..	10	10
		a. Wmk sideways		6·00	10·00
		ab. Booklet pane of 6	..	30·00	
		aw. Wmk e facing right	..	6·00	10·00
		awb. Booklet pane of 6	..	30·00	
288		1p. blue	.. ..	40	10
		a. Coil stamp. Perf 14×14½		90	60
		b. Coil strip. Nos. 288a, 289a and			
		291a *se-tenant*	..	1·50	
		c. Wmk sideways	..	35	40
		ca. Booklet pane of 6	..	2·00	
		cb. Booklet pane. No. 288c×5 plus			
		one *se-tenant* label (11.3.74)	..	2·00	
		cw. Wmk e facing right	..	35	40
		cwa. Booklet pane of 6	..	2·00	
		cwb. Booklet pane. No. 288cw×5 plus			
		one *se-tenant* label (11.3.74)	..	2·00	
289		1½p. lake-brown	..	15	15
		a. Coil stamp. Perf 14×14½		30	50
		b. Coil strip. Nos. 289a, 291a, 294a			
		and 290a *se-tenant* (24.2.72)	..	1·50	
		c. Coil strip. Nos. 289a×2, 290a			
		and 295ab *se-tenant* (29.1.74)		1·50	
290		2p. myrtle-green	..	15	10
		a. Coil stamp. Perf 14×14½			
		(24.2.72)	..	30	40
		b. Wmk sideways (27.1.75)		50	50
		ba. Booklet pane. No. 290b×5 plus			
		one *se-tenant* label	..	2·00	
		bw. Wmk e facing right	..	50	50
		bwa. Booklet pane. No. 290bw×5 plus			
		one *se-tenant* label	..	2·00	
291		2½p. sepia	..	15	10
		a. Coil stamp. Perf 14×14½			
		(20.2.71)	..	50	85
		b. Wmk sideways	..	1·00	1·25
		ba. Booklet pane of 6	..	5·50	
		bw. Wmk e facing right	..	1·00	1·25
		bwa. Booklet pane of 6	..	5·50	
292		3p. cinnamon	..	15	10
293		3½p. orange-brown	..	15	10
294		4p. pale bluish violet	..	15	10
		a. Coil stamp. Perf 14×14½			
		(24.2.72)	..	90	60
295	**91**	5p. brown and yellow-olive	..	70	20
295a	**106a**	5p. bright yellow-green (29.1.74)	..	3·50	45
		ab. Coil stamp. Perf 14×14½			
		(29.1.74)	..	1·25	90
		ac. Wmk sideways (11.3.74)	..	60	80
		ad. Booklet pane. No. 295ac×5 plus			
		one *se-tenant* label	..	2·75	
		ada. Booklet pane imperf vert	..		
		ae. Booklet pane. No. 295ac×6	..	8·00	
		awc. Wmk e facing right	..	60	80
		awd. Booklet pane. No. 295awc×5			
		plus one *se-tenant* label	..	2·75	
		awe. Booklet pane. No. 295awc×6	..	8·00	
296	**91**	6p. blackish brown and slate	..	3·50	30
296a		7p. indigo and olive-green (29.1.74)		4·00	1·00
297		7½p. chocolate and reddish lilac	..	50	85
298		9p. black and turquoise-green	..	1·00	35
299	**92**	10p. multicoloured (I)	..	18·00	10·00
299a		10p. multicoloured (II)	..	18·00	70
299b		12p. multicoloured (29.1.74)	..	75	80
300		20p. multicoloured	..	1·00	10
301	**93**	50p. multicoloured	..	2·25	65
287/301		.. .. *Set of 18*		30·00	5·25

Nos. 287a/awb, 288c/cwb, 290b/bwa, 291b/bwa and 295ac/awe

come from Booklet Nos. SB20/4. The sideways watermark has the top of the e pointing left, and the sideways inverted has it pointing right, *when seen from the back of the stamp*. Stamps with one, or two adjoining, sides imperf come from these booklets.

See also Nos. 339/59 and 478/83.

(Des H. Haflidason; adapted P. Wildbur)

1971 (3 May). *Europa. W* **22** (*sideways*). *P* 15.

302	**107**	4p. sepia and olive-yellow	..	50	10
303		6p. black and new blue..	..	1·75	2·25

108 J. M. Synge   109 "An Island Man"
(Jack B. Yeats)

(Des R. Kyne from a portrait by Jack B. Yeats)

1971 (19 July). *Birth Centenary of J. M. Synge* (*playwright*). *W* **22.** *P* 15.

304	**108**	4p. multicoloured	..	15	10
305		10p. multicoloured	..	60	80

(Des P. Wildbur)

1971 (30 Aug). *Contemporary Irish Art* (*3rd issue*). *Birth Centenary of J. B. Yeats* (*artist*). *W* **22.** *P* 15.

306	**109**	6p. multicoloured	..	55	55

110 Racial Harmony   111 "Madonna and
Symbol   Child" (statue by
                  J. Hughes)

(Des P. Wildbur. Litho Harrison)

1971 (18 Oct). *Racial Equality Year. No wmk. P* 14 × 14½.

307	**110**	4p. red ..	..	..	20	10
308		10p. black	..	..	50	75

(Des R. Kyne)

1971 (15 Nov). *Christmas. W* **22.** *P* 15.

309	**111**	2½p. black, gold and deep bluish green	10	10
310		6p. black, gold and ultramarine	..	55	65

MINIMUM PRICE

The minimum price quote is 10p which represents a handling charge rather than a basis for valuing common stamps. For further notes about prices see introductory pages.

112 Heart

(Des L. le Brocquy)

1972 (7 Apr). *World Health Day. W* **22** (*sideways*). *P* 15.

311	**112**	2½p. gold and brown	..	..	30	15
312		12p. silver and grey	..	..	1·10	1·75

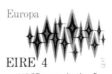

113 "Communications"

(Des P. Huovinen and P. Wildbur)

1972 (1 May). *Europa. W* **22** (*sideways*). *P* 15.

313	**113**	4p. orange, black and silver ..	..	1·25	25
314		6p. blue, black and silver	..	..	3·25	4·75

114 Dove and Moon   115 "Black Lake"
(Gerard Dillon)

(Des P. Scott)

1972 (1 June). *The Patriot Dead, 1922–23. W* **22.** *P* 15.

315	**114**	4p. grey-blue, light orange & deep blue	10	10
316		6p. dp yellow-grn, lemon & dp dull grn	45	40

(Des P. Wildbur)

1972 (10 July). *Contemporary Irish Art* (*4th issue*). *W* **22** (*sideways*). *P* 15.

317	**115**	3p. multicoloured	..	..	50	35

116 "Horseman"   117 Madonna and Child
(Carved Slab)   (from Book of Kells)

(Des P. Scott)

1972 (28 Aug). *50th Anniv of Olympic Council of Ireland.* W 22. P 15.
318	116	3p. bright yellow, black and gold	..	15	10
319		6p. salmon, black and gold	.. ..	55	60

WATERMARK. All issues from here onwards are on unwatermarked paper.

(Des P. Scott)

1972 (16 Oct). *Christmas.* P 15.
320	117	2½p. multicoloured (*shades*)	.. ..	10	10
321		4p. multicoloured	.. ..	20	10
322		12p. multicoloured	.. .. ..	55	65
320/2 ..	..	.. ..	.. *Set of 3*	75	70

118 2d. Stamp of 1922

119 Celtic Head Motif

(Des Stamping Branch of the Revenue Commissioners, Dublin)

1972 (6 Dec). *50th Anniv of the First Irish Postage Stamp.* P 15.
323	118	6p. light grey and grey-green ..	..	30	60
MS324		72 × 104 mm. No. 323 × 4	.. ..	6·50	11·00

(Des L. le Brocquy)

1973 (1 Jan). *Entry into European Communities.* P 15.
325	119	6p. multicoloured	.. ..	40	90
326		12p. multicoloured	.. ..	60	1·10

120 Europa "Posthorn"

(Des L. Anisdahl; adapted R. Kyne)

1973 (30 Apr). *Europa.* P 15.
327	120	4p. bright blue ..	.. ..	50	10
328		6p. black	.. ..	1·25	2·00

121 "Berlin Blues II" (W. Scott)

122 Weather Map

(Adapted by R. Scott)

1973 (9 Aug). *Contemporary Irish Art (5th issue).* P 15 × 14½.
329	121	5p. ultramarine and grey-black	..	40	30

(Des R. Ballagh)

1973 (4 Sept). *I.M.O./W.M.O. Centenary.* P 14½ × 15.
330	122	3½p. multicoloured	.. .. ..	30	10
331		12p. multicoloured	.. .. ..	80	2·00

123 Tractor ploughing

124 "Flight into Egypt" (Jan de Cock)

(Des P. Scott)

1973 (5 Oct). *World Ploughing Championships, Wellington Bridge.* P 15 × 14½.
332	123	5p. multicoloured	.. ..	15	10
333		7p. multicoloured	.. ..	75	50

(Des D. Kiely. Litho ("EIRE" and face value) and photo (3½p.) or photo (12p.))

1973 (1 Nov). *Christmas.* P 15.
334	124	3½p. multicoloured ..	.. ..	15	10
335		12p. multicoloured ..	.. ..	1·10	1·50

125 Daunt Island Lightship and Ballycotton Lifeboat, 1936

126 "Edmund Burke" (statue by J. H. Foley)

(Des M. Byrne from painting by B. Gribble)

1974 (28 Mar). *150th Anniv of Royal National Lifeboat Institution.* P 15 × 14½.
336	125	5p. multicoloured	.. ..	30	30

(Des P. Wildbur)

1974 (29 Apr). *Europa.* P 14½ × 15.
337	126	5p. black and pale violet-blue ..	..	75	10
338		7p. black and light emerald	..	2·50	2·50

Two types of 50p.:

Type I. Fine screen (Cyls 1)

Type II. Coarse screen (Cyls 2)

1974–83. *Designs as Nos. 287 etc. No wmk. P 15.*

339	106a	½p. bright green (5.6.78)	30	10
340		1p. blue (14.2.75)	10	10
		a. Coil stamp. Perf 14×14½ (21.3.77)	60	70
		b. Coil strip. Nos. 340a, 341a×2 and 344a *se-tenant* (21.3.77) ..	1·90	
341		2p. myrtle-green (7.4.76) ..	10	10
		a. Coil stamp. Perf 14×14½ (21.3.77)	40	50
342		3p. cinnamon (14.2.75) ..	10	10
343		3½p. orange-brown (9.10.74) ..	2·75	4·00
344		5p. bright yellow-green (16.8.74) ..	60	10
		a. Coil stamp. Perf 14 × 14½ (21.3.77)	85	1·40
345	91	6p. blackish brn & slate (16.10.74)	1·25	1·75
346	106a	6p. slate (17.6.75)	20	10
347	91	7p. indigo and olive-green (27.9.74)	90	35
348	106a	7p. deep yellow-green (17.6.75) ..	35	10
		a. Booklet pane. No. 348 × 5 plus *se-tenant* label (21.3.77) ..	11·00	
349	91	8p. dp brown & dp orge-brn (17.6.75)	75	50
350	106a	8p. chestnut (14.7.76)	30	10
351	91	9p. black & turquoise-green (12.74)	90	30
352	106a	9p. greenish slate (14.7.76) ..	30	10
352a		9½p. vermilion (3.12.79) ..	35	20
353	92	10p. multicoloured (II) (12.74) ..	2·00	30
354	91	10p. black and violet-blue (14.7.76)	1·25	10
354a	106a	10p. deep mauve (8.6.77) ..	70	10
355	91	11p. black and rose-carmine (14.7.76)	45	30
355a		12p. black and bright green (8.6.77)	75	10
355b	106a	12p. yellowish green (26.3.80) ..	30	10
355c	91	13p. reddish brn & red-brn (26.3.80)	40	1·25
356	92	15p. multicoloured (17.6.74) ..	55	40

356a	106a	15p. ultramarine (10.7.80)	40	10
356b	91	16p. black & dull yellow-grn (10.7.80)	40	80
356c	92	17p. multicoloured (8.6.77)	50	40
357		20p. multicoloured (13.6.74) ..	50	15
358	93	50p. multicoloured (I) (12.74) ..	70	30
		a. Type II (1983)	1·75	2·50
359		£1 multicoloured (17.6.75)	1·25	30
339/59		.. .. *Set of* 29	17·00	10·50

For 18p., 19p., 22p., 24p., 26p. and 29p. values printed by lithography, see Nos. 478/83.

Stamps with one or two sides imperf come from the booklet pane.

127 "Oliver Goldsmith"   **128** "Kitchen Table"
(statue by J. H. Foley)   (Norah McGuiness)

(Des P. Wildbur)

1974 (24 June). *Death Bicentenary of Oliver Goldsmith (writer).*
   P 14½ × 15.

360	127	3½p. black and olive-yellow	20	10
361		12p. black and bright yellowish green ..	90	1·00

(Design adapted by Norah McGuiness. Photo Harrison)

1974 (19 Aug). *Contemporary Irish Art (6th issue).* P 14 × 14½.

362	128	5p. multicoloured	35	30

129 Rugby Players   **130** U.P.U. "Postmark"

(Design adapted from Irish Press photograph. Eng C. Slania. Recess (3½p.) or recess and photo (12p.) Harrison)

1974 (9 Sept). *Centenary of Irish Rugby Football Union.*
   P 14½ × 14.

363	129	3½p. greenish black	30	10
		a. Deep greenish blue	7·50	3·50
364		12p. multicoloured	2·25	2·75

No. 363a is from a second printing using a recut plate on which the engraving was deeper.

(Des R. Ballagh)

1974 (9 Oct). *Centenary of Universal Postal Union.* P 14½ × 15.

365	130	5p. light yellowish green and black ..	25	10
366		7p. light ultramarine and black ..	35	80

NEW INFORMATION

The editor is always interested to correspond with people who have new information that will improve or correct the Catalogue.

131 "Madonna and Child"   **132** "Peace"
(Bellini)

(Des P. Wildbur)

1974 (14 Nov). *Christmas. P* 14½ × 15.
367 **131** 5p. multicoloured 15 10
368 15p. multicoloured 60 90

(Des Alexandra Wejchert)

1975 (24 Mar). *International Women's Year. P* 14½ × 15.
369 **132** 8p. brt reddish purple & ultramarine .. 25 75
370 15p. ultramarine and bright green .. 50 1·25

133 "Castletown Hunt" (R. Healy)

(Des R. Kyne)

1975 (28 Apr). *Europa. P* 15 × 14½.
371 **133** 7p. grey-black 75 15
372 9p. dull blue-green .. .. .. 1·25 2·50

134 Putting

(Des from photographs by J. McManus. Litho ("EIRE" and face value) and photo).

1975 (26 June). *Ninth European Amateur Golf Team Championship, Killarney. P* 15×14½.
373 **134** 6p. multicoloured (*shades*) .. 75 45
374 – 9p. multicoloured (*shades*) .. .. 1·50 1·50
The 9p. is similar to T **134** but shows a different view of the putting green.

135 "Bird of Prey" (sculpture by   **136** Nano Nagle (founder)
Oisin Kelly)   and Waifs

(Design adapted by the artist)

1975 (28 July). *Contemporary Irish Art (7th issue). P* 15×14½.
375 **135** 15p. yellow-brown 65 75

(Des Kilkenny Design Workshops)

1975 (1 Sept). *Bicentenary of Presentation Order of Nuns. P* 14½ × 15.
376 **136** 5p. black and pale blue. 20 10
377 7p. black and light stone 30 30

137 Tower of St. Anne's   **138** St. Oliver Plunkett
Church, Shandon   (commemorative medal
by Imogen Stuart)

(Des P. Scott)

1975 (6 Oct). *European Architectural Heritage Year. T* **137** *and similar vert design. P* 12½.
378 **137** 5p. blackish brown 20 10
379 6p. multicoloured 40 85
380 – 7p. steel-blue 40 10
381 – 9p. multicoloured 45 80
378/81 .. .. *Set of 4* 1·25 1·75
Design:—Nos. 380/1, Interior of Holycross Abbey, Co. Tipperary.

(Design adapted by the artist. Recess Harrison)

1975 (13 Oct). *Canonisation of Oliver Plunkett. P* 14 × 14½.
382 **138** 7p. black 15 10
383 15p. chestnut 55 45

139 "Madonna and   **140** James Larkin (from a
Child" (Fra Filippo   drawing by Sean O'Sullivan)
Lippi)

(Des P. Wildbur)

1975 (13 Nov). *Christmas. P* 15.
384 **139** 5p. multicoloured 15 10
385 7p. multicoloured 15 10
386 10p. multicoloured 45 30
384/6 .. .. *Set of 3* 65 40

(Des P. Wildbur. Litho)

1976 (21 Jan). *Birth Centenary of James Larkin (Trade Union leader). P* 14½×15.
387 **140** 7p. deep bluish green and pale grey .. 20 10
388 11p. sepia and yellow-ochre 40 55

141 Alexander Graham Bell

142 1847 Benjamin Franklin Essay

(Des R. Ballagh)

1976 (10 Mar). *Telephone Centenary. P* 14½ × 15.
389	141	9p. multicoloured	..	..	20	10
390		15p. multicoloured	..	..	45	50

(Des L. le Brocquy; graphics by P. Wildbur. Litho Irish Security Stamp Printing Ltd)

1976 (17 May). *Bicentenary of American Revolution. T* **142** *and similar horiz designs. P* 14½ × 14.
391	7p. ultramarine, light red and silver	..	15	10
	a. Silver (inscr) omitted	..	†	£225
392	8p. ultramarine, light red and silver	..	20	1·10
393	9p. violet-blue, orange and silver	..	20	10
394	15p. light rose-red, grey-blue and silver	..	30	75
	a. Silver (face-value and inscr) omitted	..	£550	£650
391/4 /..	.. ..	*Set of* 4	75	1·75
MS395	95 × 75 mm. Nos. 391/4 ..	..	4·50	8·00
	a. Silver omitted	..	£1600	

Designs:—7p. Thirteen stars; 8p. Fifty stars; 9, 15p. Type **142**.
No. **MS**395 exists with the sheet margins overprinted in blue to commemorate "Stampa 76", the Irish National Stamp Exhibition.

143 Spirit Barrel

(Des P. Hickey)

1976 (1 July). *Europa. Irish Delft. T* **143** *and similar horiz design. Multicoloured. P* 15 × 14.
396	9p. Type **143** ..	..	..	..	40	20
397	11p. Dish	..	..	..	70	1·60

144 "The Lobster Pots, West of Ireland" (Paul Henry)

(Des R. McGrath)

1976 (30 Aug). *Contemporary Irish Art* (8th issue). *P* 15.
398	144	15p. multicoloured	..	..	60	60

145 Radio Waves

(Des G. Shepherd and A. O'Donnell. Litho De La Rue Smurfit Ltd, Dublin)

1976 (5 Oct). *50th Anniv of Irish Broadcasting Service. T* **145** *and similar vert design. Chalk-surfaced paper. P* 14½×14 (9p.) *or* 14×14½ (11p.).
399	9p. light new blue and bottle-green ..	..	20	10
400	11p. agate, orange-red and light new blue	..	60	1·00

Design:—11p. Transmitter, radio waves and globe.

146 "The Nativity" (Lorenzo Monaco)

(Des R. McGrath)

1976 (11 Nov). *Christmas. P* 15×14½.
401	146	7p. multicoloured	..	..	15	10
402		9p. multicoloured	..	..	15	10
403		15p. multicoloured	..	..	55	55
401/3	..	..	..	*Set of* 3	75	65

147 16th Century Manuscript   148 Ballynahinch, Galway

(Des P. Hickey)

1977 (9 May). *Centenaries of National Library* (8p.) *and National Museum* (10p.). *T* **147** *and similar horiz design. Multicoloured. P* 15 × 14½.
404	8p. Type **147** ..	..	..	..	30	30
405	10p. Prehistoric stone ..	..	..	..	40	35

(Des E. van der Grijn. Litho Irish Security Stamp Printing Ltd)

1977 (27 June). *Europa. T* **148** *and similar vert design. Multicoloured. P* 14 × 15.
406	10p. Type **148** ..	..	..	..	30	25
407	12p. Lough Tay, Wicklow	..	..	..	95	1·50

149 "Head" (Louis le Brocquy)   150 Guide and Tents

(Design adapted by the artist. Litho Irish Security Stamp Ptg Ltd)

1977 (8 Aug). *Contemporary Irish Art* (9th issue). *P* 14 × 14½.
408	149	17p. multicoloured	..	..	55	75

(Des R. Ballagh)

1977 (22 Aug). *Scouting and Guiding.* T **150** *and similar horiz design. Multicoloured. P* 15 × 14½.

409	8p. Type **150**	..	..	..	35	10
410	17p. Tent and Scout saluting ..		..	..	75	1·75

151 "The Shanachie" (drawing by Jack B. Yeats)

152 "Electricity" (Golden Jubilee of Electricity Supply Board)

(Des L. Miller (10p.), R. Ballagh (12p.). Litho Irish Security Stamp Printing Ltd)

1977 (12 Sept). *Anniversaries.* T **151** *and similar horiz design. P* 14 × 14½ (10p.) *or* 14½ × 14 (12p.).

411	10p. black	..	..	..	25	15
412	12p. black	..	..	..	35	1·00

Designs and events:—10p. Type **151** (Golden jubilee of Irish Folklore Society; 12p. The philosopher Eriugena (1100th death anniv).

(Des R. Ballagh (10p.), P. Hickey (12p.), B. Blackshaw (17p.). Photo Stamping Branch of the Revenue Commissioners (12p.); Litho Irish Security Stamp Ptg Ltd (others))

1977 (10 Oct). *Golden Jubilees.* T **152** *and similar horiz designs. P* 15 × 14½ (12p.) *or* 15 × 14 (*others*).

413	10p. multicoloured	..	..	..	15	10
414	12p. multicoloured	..	..	..	30	1·40
415	17p. grey-black and grey-brown		..	..	40	85
413/15				*Set of 3*	75	2·10

Designs:—12p. Bulls (from contemporary coinage) (Jubilee of Agricultural Credit Corporation); 17p. Greyhound (Jubilee of greyhound track racing).

153 "The Holy Family" (Giorgione)

154 Junkers W.33 *Bremen* in Flight

(Des R. McGrath)

1977 (3 Nov). *Christmas. P* 14½ × 15.

416	**153**	8p. multicoloured	..	..	15	10
417		10p. multicoloured	..	..	15	10
418		17p. multicoloured	..	..	55	1·25
416/18		..	..	*Set of 3*	75	1·25

(Des R. Ballagh. Litho Irish Security Stamp Ptg Ltd)

1978 (13 Apr). *50th Anniv of First East–West Transatlantic Flight. P* 14 × 14½.

419	**154**	10p. bright blue and black	..	..	20	15
420	–	17p. olive-brown and black	..	..	35	1·10

The 17p. is as T **154**, but shows a different sky and sea.

155 Spring Gentian

156 Catherine McAuley

(Des Wendy Walsh. Litho Irish Security Stamp Ptg Ltd)

1978 (12 June). *Wild Flowers.* T **155** *and similar vert designs. Multicoloured. P* 14 × 15.

421	8p. Type **155** ..		..	..	25	50
422	10p. Strawberry tree ..	..		..	30	15
423	11p. Large-flowered Butterwort		..	..	35	70
424	17p. St. Dabeoc's Heath		..	..	50	2·00
421/4 ..		..	..	*Set of 4*	1·25	3·00

(Des R. Ballagh (10p.), R. Kyne (11p.), E. van der Grijn (17p.). Litho Irish Security Stamp Ptg Ltd)

1978 (18 Sept). *Anniversaries and Events.* T **156** *and similar multicoloured designs. P* 14½ × 14 (11p.) *or* 14 × 14½ (*others*).

425	10p. Type **156** ..		..	..	20	10
426	11p. Doctor performing vaccination (*horiz*)	..		30	80
427	17p. "Self Portrait"		..	..	40	1·10
425/7 ..			..	*Set of 3*	80	1·75

Events:—10p. Birth bicentenary of Catherine McAuley (founder of Sisters of Mercy); 11p. Global eradication of Smallpox; 17p. Birth centenary of Sir William Orpen (painter).

157 Diagram of Drilling Rig

158 Farthing

(Des R. Ballagh. Litho Irish Security Stamp Ptg Ltd)

1978 (18 Oct). *Arrival Onshore of Natural Gas. P* 14 × 14½.

428	**157**	10p. maroon, turquoise-green and bistre	30	30

(Des P. Wildbur and R. Mercer)

1978 (26 Oct). *50th Anniv of Irish Currency.* T **158** *and similar horiz designs. P* 15 × 14½.

429	8p. black, copper and deep bluish green		..	20	20
430	10p. black, silver and blue-green	..	..	25	10
431	11p. black, copper and chocolate	..	..	25	50
432	17p. black, silver and deep blue		..	40	1·00
429/32	..	..	..	*Set of 4*	1·00	1·60

Designs:—10p. Florin; 11p. Penny; 17p. Half-crown.

159 "The Virgin and Child" (Guercino)

160 Conolly Folly, Castletown

(Des P. Wildbur)

1978 (16 Nov).   *Christmas. P* 14½ × 15.

433	**159**	8p. purple-brown, gold and pale turquoise-green	15	10
434		10p. purple-brown, chocolate and pale turquoise-green	15	10
435		17p. purple-brown, deep blue-green and pale turquoise-green	45	1·40
433/5		*Set of 3*	65	1·40

(Des R. McGrath)

1978 (6 Dec).   *Europa. Architecture. T* **160** *and similar horiz design. P* 15 × 14½.

436	10p. lake-brown and red-brown	30	15
437	11p. green and deep green	30	1·00

Design:—11p. Dromoland Belvedere.

161 Athletes in Cross-country Race

162 "European Communities" (in languages of member nations)

(Des R. Mercer. Litho Irish Security Stamp Ptg Ltd)

1979 (20 Aug).   *7th World Cross-country Championships, Limerick. P* 14½ × 14.

438	**161**	8p. multicoloured	20	30

(Des P. Wildbur)

1979 (20 Aug).   *First Direct Elections to European Assembly. P* 14½ × 15.

439	**162**	10p. dull turquoise-green	15	15
440		11p. reddish violet	15	35

163 Sir Rowland Hill

164 Winter Wren (*Troglodytes troglodytes*)

(Des C. Harrison. Litho Irish Security Stamp Ptg Ltd)

1979 (20 Aug).   *Death Centenary of Sir Rowland Hill. P* 14 × 14½.

441	**163**	17p. black, brownish grey and red	30	60

(Des Wendy Walsh. Litho Irish Security Stamp Ptg Ltd)

1979 (30 Aug).   *Birds. T* **164** *and similar horiz designs. Multi-coloured. P* 14½ × 14.

442	8p. Type **164**	40	70
443	10p. Great Crested Grebe (*Podiceps cristatus*)	40	15
444	11p. White-fronted Goose (*Anser albifrons flavirostris*)	45	70
445	17p. Peregrine Falcon (*Falco peregrinus*)	70	2·00
442/5	*Set of 4*	1·75	3·25

165 "A Happy Flower" (David Gallagher)

(Des P. Wildbur. Litho Irish Security Stamp Ptg Ltd)

1979 (13 Sept).   *International Year of the Child. Paintings by Children. T* **165** *and similar multicoloured designs. P* 14 × 14½ (11p.) *or* 14½ × 14 (*others*).

446	10p. Type **165**	20	10
447	11p. "Myself and My Skipping Rope" (Lucy Norman) (*vert*)	25	60
448	17p. "Swans on a Lake" (Nicola O'Dwyer)	35	85
446/8	*Set of 3*	70	1·40

166 Pope John Paul II

(Des P. Byrne. Litho Irish Security Stamp Ptg Ltd)

1979 (29 Sept).   *Visit of Pope John Paul II. P* 14½ × 14.

449	**166**	12p. multicoloured	30	20

167 Brother and Child

(Des R. Kyne (9½p.), P. Scott (11p.), R. Mercer (20p.). Photo Stamping Branch of the Revenue Commissioners, Dublin (11p.), Litho Irish Security Stamp Ptg Ltd (others))

1979 (4 Oct).   *Commemorations. T* **167** *and similar designs. P* 14½ × 14 (9½p.), 14½ × 15 (11p.) *or* 14 × 14½ (*others*).

450	9½p. black and pale claret	20	10
451	11p. black, reddish orange and bright blue	20	70
452	20p. multicoloured	40	1·40
450/2	*Set of 3*	70	2·00

Designs and commemorations: *Horiz*—9½p. Type **167** (Centenary of Hospitaller Order of St. John of God in Ireland); 20p. "Seated Figure" (sculpture by F. E. McWilliam) (Contemporary Irish Art (10th issue)). *Vert*—11p. Windmill and Sun (International Energy Conservation Month).

168 Patrick Pearse, "Liberty" and General Post Office, Dublin

169 Madonna and Child (panel painting from Domnach Airgid Shrine)

(Des R. Ballagh)

1979 (10 Nov). *Birth Centenary of Patrick Pearse (patriot).*
P 15 × 14½.

453	**168**	12p. multicoloured	..	..	..	30	15

(Des Ewa Gargulinska)

1979 (15 Nov). *Christmas. P* 14½ × 15.

454	**169**	9½p. multicoloured	..	..	..	15	10
455		20p. multicoloured	..	..	..	30	55

170 Bianconi Long Car, 1836

171 John Baptist de la Salle (founder)

(Des P. Wildbur. Litho Irish Security Stamp Ptg Ltd)

1979 (6 Dec). *Europa. Communications. T* **170** *and similar horiz design. Multicoloured. P* 14½ × 14.

456	12p. Type **170**	..	..	20	30
457	13p. Transatlantic cable, Valentia, 1866	..	30	1·40

(Des P. Wildbur. Litho Irish Security Stamp Ptg Ltd)

1980 (19 Mar). *Centenary of arrival of De La Salle Order. P* 14 × 14½.

458	**171**	12p. multicoloured	..	..	30	30

172 George Bernard Shaw

173 Stoat

(Des P. Byrne. Litho Irish Security Stamp Ptg Ltd)

1980 (7 May). *Europa. Personalities. T* **172** *and similar multicoloured design. P* 14 × 14½.

459	12p. Type **173**	..	..	..	40	50
460	13p. Oscar Wilde (28 × 38 *mm*)	..	..	40	1·00

(Des Wendy Walsh. Litho Irish Security Stamp Ptg Ltd)

1980 (30 July). *Wildlife. T* **173** *and similar vert designs. Multicoloured. P* 14 × 14½.

461	12p. Type **173**	..	..	..	20	40
462	15p. Arctic Hare	..	..	..	25	15
463	16p. Red Fox	..	..	..	25	60
464	25p. Red Deer	..	..	..	40	1·60
461/4	..	..	..	*Set of* 4	1·00	2·50
MS465	73 × 97 mm. Nos. 461/4	..	..	1·25	3·00

No. **MS**465 exists with the sheet margins overprinted to commemorate "STAMPA 80", the Irish National Stamp Exhibition, in black or red, and for the Dublin Stamp Show, 1992, in red.

174 Playing Bodhran and Whistle   175 Sean O'Casey

(Des J. Dixon and P. Wildbur. Litho Irish Security Stamp Ptg Ltd)

1980 (25 Sept). *Traditional Music and Dance. T* **174** *and similar vert designs. Multicoloured. P* 14 × 14½.

466	12p. Type **174**	..	..	..	15	10
467	15p. Playing Uilleann pipes	..	..	20	15
468	25p. Dancing	..	..	..	35	1·10
466/8	..	..	..	*Set of* 3	65	1·25

(Des P. Wildbur (12p.), P. Scott (25p.). Litho Irish Security Stamp Ptg Ltd)

1980 (23 Oct). *Commemorations. T* **175** *and similar vert design. P* 14 × 14½.

469	12p. multicoloured	..	..	..	15	10
470	25p. black, buff and drab	..	..	30	55

Designs and commemorations:—12p. Type **175** (Birth centenary of Sean O'Casey (playwright)); 25p. "Gold Painting No. 57" (Patrick Scott) (Contemporary Irish Art (11th issue)).

176 Nativity Scene (painting by Geraldine McNulty)   177 Boyle Air-pump, 1659

(Des P. Wildbur)

1980 (13 Nov). *Christmas. P* 14½ × 15.

471	**176**	12p. multicoloured	..	..	15	10
472		15p. multicoloured	..	..	20	10
473		25p. multicoloured	..	..	40	1·25
471/3	..	..	..	*Set of* 3	65	1·25

(Des P. Wildbur. Litho Irish Security Stamp Ptg Ltd)

1981 (12 Mar). *Irish Science and Technology. T* **177** *and similar vert designs. Multicoloured. P* 14 × 14½.

474	12p. Type **177**	..	..	..	20	10
475	15p. Ferguson tractor, 1936	..	..	25	10
476	16p. Parsons turbine, 1884	..	..	25	90
477	25p. Holland submarine, 1878	..	..	30	1·25
474/7	..	..	..	*Set of* 4	90	2·10

(Litho Irish Security Stamp Ptg Ltd)

1981 (27 Apr)**–82**. *No wmk. P* 14 × 14½.

478	**106***a*	18p. dull claret	..	..	45	50
479		19p. light blue	..	..	55	1·75
480		22p. dull turquoise-blue (1.9.81)	..	65	10
481		24p. drab (29.10.81)	..	..	75	95
482		26p. blue-green (1.4.82)	..	..	1·50	40
483		29p. purple (1.4.82)	..	..	1·75	2·00
478/83	..	..	..	*Set of* 6	5·00	5·00

178 "The Legend of   **179** Cycling
the Cock and the Pot"

(Des P. Byrne. Litho Irish Security Stamp Ptg Ltd)

1981 (4 May). *Europa. Folklore. Paintings by Maria Simonds-
Gooding. T* **178** *and similar vert design. P* 14 × 14½.
491   18p. black, orange-yellow and carmine   25   10
492   19p. black, yellow-orange and yellow   ..   35   70
Design:—19p. "The Angel with the Scales of Judgement".

(Des R. Ballagh. Litho Irish Security Stamp Ptg Ltd)

1981 (24 June). *50th Anniv of "An Óige" (Irish Youth Hostel
Association). T* **179** *and similar multicoloured designs.
P* 14 × 14½ (15, 30p.) *or* 14½ × 14 (*others*).
493   15p. Type **179**   30   40
494   18p. Hill-walking (*horiz*)   30   10
495   19p. Mountaineering (*horiz*)   30   95
496   30p. Rock-climbing   50   95
493/6 ..   ..   *Set of* 4 1·25   2·25

180 Jeremiah   **181** "Railway Embankment"
O'Donovan Rossa   (W. J. Leech)

(Des C. Harrison. Litho Irish Security Stamp Ptg Ltd)

1981 (31 Aug). *150th Birth Anniv of Jeremiah O'Donovan Rossa
(politician). P* 14 × 14½.
497   **180**   15p. multicoloured   30   30

(Des P. Wildbur. Litho Irish Security Stamp Ptg Ltd)

1981 (31 Aug). *Contemporary Irish Art (12th issue). P* 14½ × 14.
498   **181**   30p. multicoloured   60   60

182 James Hoban and   **183** "Arkle" (steeplechaser)
White House

(Des B. Thompson. Litho Irish Security Stamp Ptg Ltd)

1981 (29 Sept). *150th Death Anniv of James Hoban (White House
architect). P* 14 × 14½.
499   **182**   18p. multicoloured   30   30

(Des Wendy Walsh and P. Wildbur. Litho Irish Security Stamp Ptg
Ltd)

1981 (23 Oct). *Famous Irish Horses. T* **183** *and similar horiz
designs. Multicoloured. Ordinary paper* (18p.) *or chalk-surfaced paper* (*others*). *P* 14½ × 14.
500   18p. Type **183**   40   1·00
      a. Pair. Nos. 500/1   80   2·00
501   18p. "Boomerang" (showjumper)   40   1·00
502   22p. "King of Diamonds" (Draught horse)   ..   40   30
503   24p. "Ballymoss" (flatracer)   40   70
504   36p. "Coosheen Finn" (Connemara pony)   ..   60   1·00
500/4   ..   ..   *Set of* 5 2·00   3·50
The 18p values were printed together, *se-tenant,* in horizontal
and vertical pairs throughout the sheet.

184 "Nativity" (F. Barocci)   **185** Eviction Scene

(Des P. Wildbur. Litho Irish Security Stamp Ptg Ltd)

1981 (19 Nov). *Christmas. Chalk-surfaced paper. P* 14 × 14½.
505   **184**   18p. multicoloured   20   10
506   22p. multicoloured   25   10
507   36p. multicoloured   45   2·00
505/7 ..   ..   *Set of* 3   80   2·00

(Des R. Mercer (18p.), P. Wildbur (22p.). Litho Irish Security Stamp
Ptg Ltd)

1981 (10 Dec). *Anniversaries. T* **185** *and similar multicoloured
design. Chalk-surfaced paper. P* 14 × 14½ (18p.) *or* 14½ × 14
(22p.).
508   18p. Type **185**   35   25
509   22p. Royal Dublin Society emblem (*horiz*) ..   40   30
Anniversaries—18p. Centenary of Land Law (Ireland) Act; 22p.
250th of Royal Dublin Society (organization for the advancement
of agriculture, industry, art and science).

186 Upper Lake, Killarney   **187** "The Stigmatization
National Park   of St Francis" (Sassetta)

(Des P. Wildbur. Litho Irish Security Stamp Ptg Ltd)

1982 (26 Feb). *50th Anniv of Killarney National Park. T* **186** *and
similar horiz design. Multicoloured. P* 14½ × 14.
510   18p. Type **186**   35   20
511   36p. Eagle's Nest   65   1·60

(Des P. Wildbur (22p.), M. Craig (24p.). Litho Irish Security Stamp
Ptg Ltd)

1982 (2 Apr). *Religious Anniversaries. T* **187** *and similar horiz
design. Chalk-surfaced paper. P* 14 × 14½ (22p.) *or* 14½ × 14
(24p.).
512   22p. multicoloured   35   15
513   24p. olive-brown   40   80
Designs and anniversaries:—22p. Type **187** (800th birth anniv
of St Francis of Assisi (founder of Franciscan Order)); 24p.
Francis Makemie (founder of American Presbyterianism) and
old Presbyterian Church, Ramelton, Co Donegal (300th anniv of
ordination).

ÉIRE 26

188 The Great Famine,   **189** Pádraic Ó Conaire
1845–50   (writer) (Birth Centenary)

(Des P. Wildbur. Litho Irish Security Stamp Ptg Ltd)

1982 (4 May). *Europa. Historic Events.* T **188** *and similar design. Chalk-surfaced paper.* P 14 × 14½ (26p.) *or* 14½ × 14 (29p.).

514	26p. black and stone	..	80	50
515	29p. multicoloured	..	80	2·00

Design: *Horiz*—29p. The coming of Christianity to Ireland.

(Des P. Wildbur. Litho Irish Security Stamp Ptg Ltd)

1982 (16 June). *Anniversaries of Cultural Figures.* T **189** *and similar vert designs. Chalk-surfaced paper.* P 14 × 14½.

516	22p. black and light blue	..	25	30
517	26p. black and sepia	..	30	30
518	29p. black and blue	..	40	1·25
519	44p. black and greenish grey	..	50	1·75
516/19		*Set of* 4	1·25	3·25

Designs and anniversaries—26p. James Joyce (writer) (Birth centenary); 29p. John Field (musician) (Birth bicentenary); 44p. Charles Kickham (writer) (Death centenary).

22 ÉIRE

ÉIRE 22

190 Porbeagle Shark   **191** *St. Patrick*
(*Lamna nasus*)   (Galway hooker)

(Des Wendy Walsh and P. Wildbur. Litho Irish Security Stamp Ptg Ltd)

1982 (29 July). *Marine Life.* T **190** *and similar horiz designs. Multicoloured. Chalk-surfaced paper.* P 14½ × 14.

520	22p. Type **190**	..	55	1·25
521	22p. Common European Oyster (*Ostrea edulis*)	..	55	1·25
522	26p. Atlantic Salmon (*Salmo salar*)	..	70	30
523	29p. Dublin Bay Prawn (*Nephrops norvegicus*)	..	70	2·25
520/3		*Set of* 4	2·25	4·50

(Des P. Wildbur. Litho Irish Security Stamp Ptg Ltd)

1982 (21 Sept). *Irish Boats.* T **191** *and similar multicoloured designs. *Ordinary paper* (26p.) *or chalk-surfaced paper* (*others*). P 14 × 14½ (*Nos.* 524 *and* 527) *or* 14½ × 14 (*others*).

524	22p. Type **191**	..	60	1·25
525	22p. Currach (*horiz*)	..	60	1·25
526	26p. *Asgard II* (cadet brigantine) (*horiz*)	..	60	30
527	29p. Howth 17 foot yacht	..	60	2·25
524/7		*Set of* 4	2·25	4·50

192 "Irish House of Commons"   **193** "Madonna and Child"
(painting by Francis Wheatley)   (sculpture)

(Des P. Wildbur (22p.) or R. Ballagh (26p.). Litho Irish Security Stamp Ptg Ltd)

1982 (14 Oct). *Bicentenary of Grattan's Parliament* (22p.) *and Birth Centenary of Éamon de Valera* (26p.). T **192** *and similar multicoloured design.* P 14½ × 14 (22p.) *or* 14 × 14½ (26p.).

528	22p. Type **192**	..	35	1·25
529	26p. Éamon de Valera (*vert*)	..	40	40

(Des P. Wildbur. Litho Irish Security Stamp Ptg Ltd)

1982 (11 Nov). *Christmas.* P 14 × 14½.

530	**193** 22p. multicoloured	..	30	90
531	26p. multicoloured	..	30	35

EIRE 22

194 Aughnanure Castle   **195** Ouzel Galley Goblet

(Des M. Craig and P. Wildbur. Litho Irish Security Stamp Ptg Ltd)

1982 (15 Dec)–**90**. *Irish Architecture.* T **194** *and similar designs. Chalk-surfaced paper* (24, 28, 32, 37, 39, 46p., £1 (*No.* 550b), £2) *or ordinary paper* (*others*). P 15×14 (15, 20, 22, 23, 24, 26, 39, 46, 50p., £1 (*No.* 550), £2, £5) *or* 14×15 (*others*).

532	1p. dull violet-blue (6.7.83)	..	10	10
	a. Chalk-surfaced paper (9.87)	..	40	40
533	2p. deep yellow-green (6.7.83)	..	20	10
	a. Chalk-surfaced paper (27.6.85)	..	50	40
	ab. Booklet pane. Nos. 533a, 543a and 545a, each × 2	..	5·50	
	ac. Booklet pane. Nos. 533a, 543a and 545a, each × 4	..	9·00	
	ad. Booklet pane. Nos. 533a×2, 535b×3, 544a×3 and 545c×4 (8.9.86)	..	9·00	
	ae. Booklet pane. Nos. 533a×4, 535b, 544a×2 and 545c×5 (24.11.88)	..	10·00	
534	3p. black (6.7.83)	..	20	10
	a. Chalk-surfaced paper (2.88)	..	90	90
535	4p. maroon (16.3.83)	..	20	10
	a. Booklet pane. Nos. 535×3, 543×4 and 1 label (15.8.83)	..	2·50	
	b. Chalk-surfaced paper (9.7.84)	..	40	40
	ba. Booklet pane. Nos. 535b×3, 543a×5 and 545a×4	..	6·50	
	c. Perf 13½ (3.5.90)	..	4·00	4·00
	ca. Booklet pane. Nos. 535c×3, 545b, 752ab×2 and 754ab×2	..	30·00	
536	5p. olive-sepia (6.7.83)	..	30	10
	a. Chalk-surfaced paper (8.87)	..	70	30
537	6p. deep grey-blue (16.3.83)	..	30	15
	a. Chalk-surfaced paper (11.85)	..	1·75	1·75
538	7p. dull yellow-green (16.3.83)	..	30	15
	a. Chalk-surfaced paper (3.88)	..	2·00	2·00
539	10p. black (6.7.83)	..	30	10
	a. Chalk-surfaced paper (3.87)	..	85	30
540	12p. purple-brown (6.7.83)	..	30	30
	a. Chalk-surfaced paper (5.87)	..	3·25	3·25

541	15p. deep yellow-green (6.7.83)	..	45	35
542	20p. deep brown-purple (16.3.83)	..	50	45
	a. Chalk-surfaced paper (12.84)	..	1·75	1·75
543	22p. chalky blue ..	..	50	10
	a. Chalk-surfaced paper (9.7.84)	..	1·75	50
544	23p. yellow-green (16.3.83)	..	85	80
544a	24p. bistre-brown (27.6.85)	..	1·25	35
	ab. Ordinary paper (9.87)	..	3·25	2·00
545	26p. blackish brown	..	75	10
	a. Chalk-surfaced paper (9.7.84)	..	1·25	30
	b. Perf 13½ (3.5.90)	..	5·00	5·00
545c	28p. maroon (27.6.85)	..	75	45
	ca. Ordinary paper (10.87)	..	9·00	9·00
546	29p. deep yellow-green	..	90	65
547	30p. black (16.3.83)	..	70	30
	a. Chalk-surfaced paper (3.87)	..	70	90
	b. Perf 13½ (3.5.90)	..	6·00	6·00
	ba. Booklet pane. Nos. 547b, 754ab and 774a/5a		12·00	
	bb. Booklet pane. Nos. 547b×2, 754ab×2 and 774a		15·00	
547c	32p. bistre-brown (1.5.86)	..	1·75	2·25
	ca. Ordinary paper (9.90)	..	5·00	7·00
547d	37p. chalky blue (27.6.85)	..	90	1·60
547e	39p. maroon (1.5.86)	..	1·75	2·25
548	44p. black and grey	..	90	90
	a. Chalk-surfaced paper (4.85)	..	3·00	3·00
548b	46p. olive-green and brownish grey (1.5.86)		4·00	2·00
	ba. Ordinary paper (9.87)	..	15·00	15·00
549	50p. dull ultramarine and grey (16.3.83)		1·00	65
	a. Chalk-surfaced paper (12.84)	..	2·50	90
550	£1 bistre-brown and grey	..	3·75	3·00
	a. Chalk-surfaced paper (9.84)	..	10·00	7·50
550b	£1 chalky blue & brownish grey (27.6.85)		3·25	1·25
	ba. Ordinary paper (1.88)	..	16·00	16·00
550c	£2 grey-olive and black (26.7.88)	..	4·00	4·50
551	£5 crimson and grey	..	10·00	5·00
	a. Chalk-surfaced paper (8.87)	..	30·00	30·00
532/51		Set of 28	35·00	24·00

Designs: *Horiz (as T 194)*—1p. to 5p. Central Pavilion, Dublin Botanic Gardens; 6p. to 12p. Dr. Steevens' Hospital, Dublin; 28p. to 37p. St. MacDara's Church. (37×21 *mm*)—46p., £1 (No. 550) Cahir Castle: 50p., £2 Casino, Marino; £5 Central Bus Station, Dublin. *Vert (as T 194)*— 15p. to 22p. Type 194; 23p. to 26p., 39p. Cormac's Chapel. (21×37 *mm*)—44p., £1 (No. 550b) Killarney Cathedral.

The following stamps first appeared in booklet panes, but were later issued in sheets: Nos. 533a (7.86), 535b (7.85), 543a (10.84) and 545a (1.85).

Nos. 533ab/ae and 535a/ba show the horizontal edges of the panes imperforate so that 2, 22 and 26p. values from them exist imperforate at top, bottom, left or right, the 4p. at top or bottom the 24p. at right and the 28p. at top.

No. 535ba comes from a £2 Discount booklet and shows "Booklet Stamp" printed over the gum on the reverse of each stamp.

Nos. 535c, 545b and 547b are on ordinary paper and come from the 1990 150th Anniversary of the Penny Black £6 booklet. Examples of Nos. 535c, 545b and 752ab from the right-hand column of booklet pane No. 535ca are imperforate at right (4p.) or top (others). In booklet pane No. 547bb Nos. 547b and 754ab are imperforate at right.

Booklet pane No. 547ba exists with the margins overprinted to commemorate "New Zealand 1990" International Stamp Exhibition Auckland, and No. 547bb with the margins overprinted in blue for "STAMPA 90", the Irish National Stamp Exhibition.

Nos. 550/a were withdrawn without warning on 14 November 1984 after the authorities had discovered forged examples of the £1 stamp used in P.O. savings books. Such forgeries, which it is believed were not used for postal purposes, are line perforated 14.75 or 12 instead of the 14.75×14 comb perforation of the genuine and also show the foot of the "1" rounded instead of square.

(Des P. Wildbur (22p.), C. Harrison (26p.). Litho Irish Security Stamp Ptg Ltd)

1983 (23 Feb). *Bicentenaries of Dublin Chamber of Commerce (22p.) and Bank of Ireland (26p.). T 195 and similar multicoloured design. P 14 × 14½ (22p.) or 14½ × 14 (26p.).*

552	22p. Type 195	..	30	55
553	26p. Bank of Ireland building (*horiz*)..	..	35	35

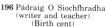

196 Pádraig O Siochfhradha (writer and teacher) (Birth cent)

197 Neolithic Carved Pattern, Newgrange Tomb

(Des C. Harrison (26p.), R. Ballagh (29p.). Litho Irish Security Stamp Ptg Ltd)

1983 (7 Apr). *Anniversaries. T 196 and similar vert design. Multicoloured. P 14 × 14½.*

554	26p. Type 196	..	50	75
555	29p. Young Boys' Brigade member (Centenary)	.. ..	60	1·50

(Des L. le Brocquy (26p.), P. Wildbur (29p.). Litho Irish Security Stamp Ptg Ltd)

1983 (4 May). *Europa. T 197 and similar horiz design. P 14½ × 14.*

556	26p. grey-black and gold	..	1·75	50
557	29p. black, blackish brown and gold ..	..	4·00	5·00

Design:—29p. Sir William Rowan Hamilton's formulae for the multiplication of quaternions.

198 Kerry Blue Terrier

(Des Wendy Walsh and L. Miller. Litho Irish Security Stamp Ptg Ltd)

1983 (23 June). *Irish Dogs. T 198 and similar horiz designs. Multicoloured. P 14½ × 14.*

558	22p. Type 198	.. ..	65	35
559	26p. Irish Wolfhound ..	.. ..	75	45
560	26p. Irish Water Spaniel	.. ..	75	45
561	29p. Irish Terrier	.. ..	95	2·25
562	44p. Irish Setters	.. ..	1·40	2·50
558/62		Set of 5	4·00	5·50
MS563	142 × 80 mm. Nos. 558/62 ..	..	6·00	8·00

No. **MS**563 exists with the sheet margins overprinted in blue to commemorate "STAMPA 83", the Irish National Stamp Exhibition.

199 Animals (Irish Society for the Prevention of Cruelty to Animals)

200 Postman with Bicycle

(Des Wendy Walsh (No. 564), B. Murphy (No. 566), K. Uhlemann (No. 567), R. Ballagh (others). Litho Irish Security Stamp Ptg Ltd)

1983 (11 Aug). *Anniversaries and Commemorations. T* **199** *and similar designs.* P 14½ × 14 (*Nos.* 564, 566) *or* 14 × 14½ (*others*).

564	**199**	22p. multicoloured	..	..	50	1·00
565	–	22p. multicoloured	..	..	50	1·00
566	–	26p. multicoloured	..	..	50	60
567	–	26p. multicoloured	..	..	50	60
568	–	44p. grey-blue and black	..	..	75	2·00
564/8	..	.. .. ..	*Set of* 5		2·50	4·75

Designs: *Vert*—No. 565, Sean Mac Diarmada (patriot) (Birth cent); No. 567, "St. Vincent de Paul in the Streets of Paris" (150th anniv of Society of St. Vincent de Paul); No. 568, "Andrew Jackson" (Frank McKelvey) (President of the United States). *Horiz*—No. 566, "100" (Centenary of Industrial Credit Company).

(Des R. Ballagh. Litho Irish Security Stamp Ptg Ltd)

1983 (15 Sept). *World Communications Year. T* **200** *and similar vert design. Multicoloured.* P 14 × 14½.

569	22p. Type **200**	..	..	..	55	75
570	29p. Dish antenna	..	..	..	70	2·00

201 Weaving

202 "La Natividad" (R. van der Weyden)

(Des R. Mercer. Litho Irish Security Stamp Ptg Ltd)

1983 (13 Oct). *Irish Handicrafts. T* **201** *and similar vert designs. Multicoloured.* P 14 × 14½.

571	22p. Type **201**	..	..	..	40	50
572	26p. Basketmaking	..	..	..	40	35
573	29p. Irish crochet	..	..	..	45	1·25
574	44p. Harpmaking	..	..	..	70	2·00
571/4	.. ..	*Set of* 4			1·75	3·50

(Des and litho Irish Security Stamp Ptg Ltd)

1983 (30 Nov). *Christmas.* P 14 × 14½.

575	**202**	22p. multicoloured	..	..	35	30
576		26p. multicoloured	..	..	40	30

203 Dublin and Kingstown Railway Steam Locomotive *Princess*

(Des C. Rycroft. Litho Irish Security Stamp Ptg Ltd)

1984 (30 Jan). *150th Anniv of Irish Railways. T* **203** *and similar horiz designs. Multicoloured. Ordinary paper* (23p., 26p. *and miniature sheet*) *or chalk-surfaced paper* (*others*). P 15×14.

577	23p. Type **203**	..	..	75	1·25
578	26p. Great Southern Railway steam locomotive *Macha*	..	..	75	35
579	29p. Great Northern Railway steam locomotive No. 87 *Kestrel*	..	..	85	1·75

580	44p. Coras Iompair Eireann two-car electric unit	..	..	1·10	2·25
577/80	.. ..		*Set of* 4	3·00	5·00
MS581	129×77 mm. Nos. 577/80		..	4·75	7·00

No. **MS**581 exists with the sheet margins overprinted in black to commemorate "STAMPA 84", the Irish National Stamp Exhibition.

204 *Sorbus hibernica*

(Des Wendy Walsh and P. Wildbur. Litho Irish Security Stamp Ptg Ltd)

1984 (1 Mar). *Irish Trees. T* **204** *and similar horiz designs. Multicoloured.* P 15 × 14.

582	22p. Type **204**	..	..	..	65	70
583	26p. *Taxus baccata fastigiata*	..	..	70	40
584	29p. *Salix hibernica*	..	..	85	2·00
585	44p. *Betula pubescens*	..	..	1·10	2·75
582/5	.. ..	*Set of* 4			3·00	5·25

205 St. Vincent's Hospital, Dublin

(Des B. Donegan, adapted by C. Vis (26p.), B. Murphy (44p.). Litho Irish Security Stamp Ptg Ltd)

1984 (12 Apr). *150th Anniv of St. Vincent's Hospital and Bicentenary of Royal College of Surgeons. T* **205** *and similar horiz design. Multicoloured.* P 15 × 14.

586	26p. Type **205**	..	..	50	30
587	44p. Royal College and logo	..	..	90	1·50

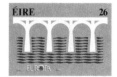

206 C.E.P.T. 25th Anniversary Logo

(Des J. Larrivière. Litho Irish Security Stamp Ptg Ltd)

1984 (10 May). *Europa.* P 15 × 14.

588	**206**	26p. blue, deep dull blue and black	..	1·75	50
589		29p. light green, blue-green and black	..	2·25	2·75

207 Flags on Ballot Box

208 John McCormack

(Des R. Ballagh. Litho Irish Security Stamp Ptg Ltd)

1984 (10 May). *Second Direct Elections to European Assembly.*
P 15 × 14.
590 **207** 26p. multicoloured   50   70

(Des R. Mercer and J. Sharpe. Litho Irish Security Stamp Ptg Ltd)

1984 (6 June). *Birth Centenary of John McCormack (tenor).*
P 14 × 15.
591 **208** 22p. multicoloured   50   70

209 Hammer-throwing

(Des L. le Brocquy and P. Wildbur. Litho Irish Security Stamp
Ptg Ltd)

1984 (21 June). *Olympic Games, Los Angeles. T* **209** *and*
similar horiz designs. P 15 × 14.
592 22p. deep mauve, black and gold   ..   35   80
593 26p. violet, black and gold   ..   40   65
594 29p. bright blue, black and gold   ..   60   1·25
592/4 ..   ..   *Set of* 3   1·25   2·50
Designs:—26p. Hurdling; 29p. Running.

210 Hurling   211 Galway Mayoral Chain (500th
                  Anniv of Mayoral Charter)

(Des C. Harrison. Litho Irish Security Stamp Ptg Ltd)

1984 (23 Aug). *Centenary of Gaelic Athletic Association. T* **210**
and similar multicoloured design. P 15 × 14 (22p.) *or* 14 × 15
(26p.).
595 22p. Type **210**   50   90
596 26p. Irish football (*vert*)   60   90

(Des P. Wildbur. Litho Irish Security Stamp Ptg Ltd)

1984 (18 Sept). *Anniversaries. T* **211** *and similar multicoloured*
design. P 14 × 15 (26p.) *or* 15 × 14 (44p.).
597 26p. Type **211**   35   50
598 44p. St. Brendan (from 15th-cent Bodleian
manuscript) (1500th birth anniv) (*horiz*)   75   1·50

212 Hands passing Letter   213 "Virgin and Child"
                            (Sassoferrato)

(Litho Irish Security Stamp Ptg Ltd)

1984 (19 Oct). *Bicentenary of the Irish Post Office. P* 15 × 14.
599 **212** 26p. multicoloured   60   70

(Des O'Connor O'Sullivan Advertising (17p.), P. Wildbur (others).
Litho Irish Security Stamp Ptg Ltd)

1984 (26 Nov). *Christmas. T* **213** *and similar multicoloured*
design. Chalk-surfaced paper. P 15 × 14 (17p.) *or* 14 × 15
(*others*).
600 17p. Christmas star (*horiz*)   ..   45   80
601 22p. Type **213**   45   1·25
602 26p. Type **213**   65   40
600/2 ..   ..   *Set of* 3   1·40   2·25
No. 600 represented a special concession rate for Christmas card
postings to addresses within Ireland and Great Britain between 26
November and 8 December 1984.

214 "Love" and Heart-shaped   215 Dunsink Observatory
     Balloon   (Bicentenary)

(Des Susan Dubsky (22p.), Patricia Jorgensen (26p.). Litho Irish
Security Stamp Ptg Ltd)

1985 (31 Jan). *Greetings Stamps. T* **214** *and similar multi-*
coloured design. Chalk-surfaced paper. P 15 × 14 (22p.) *or*
14 × 15 (26p.).
603 22p. Type **214**   50   75
604 26p. Bouquet of hearts and flowers (*vert*)   60   75

(Des R. Ballagh (22, 44p.), K. Thomson (26p.), M. Lunt (37p.). Litho
Irish Security Stamp Ptg Ltd)

1985 (14 Mar). *Anniversaries. T* **215** *and similar designs. Multi-*
coloured. Chalk-surfaced paper. P 15 × 14 (26p.) *or* 14 × 15
(*others*).
605 22p. Type **215**   50   50
606 26p. "A Landscape at Tivoli, Cork, with
Boats" (Nathaniel Grogan) (800th
anniv of City of Cork) (*horiz*)   ..   50   30
607 37p. Royal Irish Academy (Bicentenary) ..   70   1·75
608 44p. Richard Crosbie's balloon flight (Bicentenary of first aeronautic flight by an
Irishman)   80   1·75
605/8 ..   ..   *Set of* 4   2·25   3·75

216 *Polyommatus*   217 Charles Villiers
    icarus   Stanford (composer)

(Des I. Loe. Litho Irish Security Stamp Ptg Ltd)

1985 (11 Apr). *Butterflies. T* **216** *and similar vert designs.*
Multicoloured. Chalk-surfaced paper. P 14 × 15.
609 22p. Type **216**   ..   ..   ..   1·25   1·00
610 26p. *Vanessa atalanta*   ..   ..   1·25   70
611 28p. *Gonepteryx rhamni* ..   ..   1·50   2·75
612 44p. *Eurodryas aurinia*   ..   ..   2·00   3·00
609/12 ..   ..   *Set of* 4   5·50   6·75

(Des P. Hickey and J. Farrar. Litho Irish Security Stamp Ptg Ltd)

1985 (16 May). *Europa. Irish Composers. T* **217** *and similar horiz design. Multicoloured. Chalk-surfaced paper. P* 15×14.
613	26p. Type **217**	..	2·00	50
614	37p. Turlough Carolan (composer and lyricist)	.. ..	4·00	5·50

G.F. Handel · 1685-1759

218 George Frederick Handel

219 U.N. Patrol of Irish Soldiers, Congo, 1960 (25th Anniv. of Irish Participation in U.N. Peace-keeping Force)

(Des K. Uhlemann and J. Farrar. Litho Irish Security Stamp Ptg Ltd)

1985 (16 May). *European Music Year. Composers. T* **218** *and similar vert designs. Multicoloured. Chalk-surfaced paper. P* 14×15.
615	22p. Type **218**	.. .. ..	1·25	2·50
	a. Pair. Nos. 615/16	..	2·50	5·00
616	22p. Guiseppe Domenico Scarlatti	..	1·25	2·50
617	26p. Johann Sebastian Bach	..	1·50	50
615/17	.. ..	*Set of 3*	3·50	5·00

Nos. 615/16 were printed together, *se-tenant*, in horizontal and vertical pairs throughout the sheet.

(Des B. Donegan and J. Farrar (22p.), R. Ballagh (26p.), B. Donegan (44p.). Litho Irish Security Stamp Ptg Ltd)

1985 (20 June). *Anniversaries. T* **219** *and similar multicoloured designs. Chalk-surfaced paper. P* 15×14 (22p.) *or* 14×15 (*others*).
618	22p. Type **219**	.. ..	65	80
619	26p. Thomas Ashe (patriot) (Birth cent) (*vert*) ..	.. ..	65	60
620	44p. "Bishop George Berkeley" (James Lathan) (philosopher) (300th birth anniv) (*vert*) ..	.. ..	1·00	3·00
618/20	.. .. ..	*Set of 3*	2·10	4·00

220 Group of Young People

221 Visual Display Unit

(Des J. Farrar and N. Mooney. Litho Irish Security Stamp Ptg Ltd)

1985 (1 Aug). *International Youth Year. T* **220** *and similar multicoloured design. Chalk-surfaced paper. P* 15×14 (22p.) *or* 14×15 (26p.).
621	22p. Type **220**	.. .. ..	55	50
622	26p. Students and young workers (*vert*)	..	55	50

NEW INFORMATION

The editor is always interested to correspond with people who have new information that will improve or correct the Catalogue.

(Des B. Donegan (44p.), C. Rycraft (others). Litho Irish Security Stamp Ptg Ltd)

1985 (3 Oct). *Industrial Innovation. T* **221** *and similar horiz designs. Multicoloured. Chalk-surfaced paper. P* 15×14.
623	22p. Type **221**	..	65	75
624	26p. Turf cutting with hand tool and with modern machinery	..	70	55
625	44p. "The Key Man" (Sean Keating) (150th anniv of Institution of Engineers of Ireland) ..	.. .. ..	1·25	2·50
623/5	..	*Set of 3*	2·40	3·50

222 Lighted Candle and Holly

223 "Virgin and Child in a Landscape" (Adrian van Ijsenbrandt)

(Des R. Mahon (No. 626). Litho Irish Security Stamp Ptg Ltd)

1985 (26 Nov). *Christmas. T* **222** *and designs as T* **223** *showing paintings. Multicoloured. Chalk-surfaced paper. P* 15×14 (26p.) *or* 14×15 (*others*).
626	22p. Type **222**	.. ..	75	65
	a. Sheetlet. No. 626×16	..	11·00	
627	22p. Type **223**	.. ..	90	2·50
	a. Pair. Nos. 627/8	..	1·75	5·00
628	22p. "The Holy Family" (Murillo)	..	90	2·50
629	26p. "The Adoration of the Shepherds" (Louis le Nain) (*horiz*) ..	..	90	25
626/9	.. ..	*Set of 4*	3·00	5·50

No. 626 was only issued in sheetlets of 16 sold at £3, providing a discount of 52p. off the face value of the stamps.

Nos. 627/8 were printed together, *se-tenant*, in horizontal and vertical pairs throughout the sheet.

224 Stylised Love Bird with Letter

225 Hart's Tongue Fern

(Des R. Hoek (22p.), T. Monaghan (26p.). Litho Irish Security Stamp Ptg Ltd)

1986 (30 Jan). *Greetings Stamps. T* **224** *and similar vert design. Multicoloured. Chalk-surfaced paper. P* 14×15.
630	22p. Type **224**	.. ..	55	90
631	26p. Heart-shaped pillar-box	..	55	90

(Des I. Loe. Litho Irish Security Stamp Ptg Ltd)

1986 (20 Mar). *Ferns. T* **255** *and similar vert designs. Multicoloured. Chalk-surfaced paper. P* 14×15.
632	24p. Type **225**	.. ..	70	70
633	28p. Rusty-back Fern	.. ..	80	70
634	46p. Killarney Fern	.. ..	1·25	2·10
632/4	.. .. ..	*Set of 3*	2·50	3·25

226 "Harmony between Industry and Nature"

227 Boeing 747-200 over Globe showing Aer Lingus Routes

(Des G. van Gelderen. Litho Irish Security Stamp Ptg Ltd)

1986 (1 May). *Europa. Protection of the Environment.* T **226** *and similar multicoloured design. Chalk-surfaced paper.* P 14 × 15 (28p.) or 15 × 14 (39p.).

635	28p. Type **226**	..	..	1·75	50
636	39p. *Vanessa atalanta* (butterfly) and tractor in field ("Preserve hedgerows") (*horiz*)		..	3·25	5·00

(Des R. Ballagh. Litho Irish Security Stamp Ptg Ltd)

1986 (27 May). *50th Anniv of Aer Lingus* (airline). T **227** *and similar horiz design. Multicoloured. Chalk-surfaced paper.* P 15 × 14.

637	28p. Type **227**	..		1·40	75
638	46p. De Havilland D.H.84 Dragon Mk 2 *Iolar* (first aircraft)		..	1·90	3·00

228 Grand Canal at Robertstown

229 *Severn* (19th-century paddle-steamer)

(Des B. Matthews. Litho Irish Security Stamp Ptg Ltd)

1986 (27 May). *Irish Waterways.* T **228** *and similar multicoloured designs. Chalk-surfaced paper.* P 14 × 15 (28p.) or 15 × 14 (others).

639	24p. Type **228**	..	..	1·00	1·00
640	28p. Fishing in County Mayo (*vert*)	..	..	1·25	1·00
641	30p. Motor cruiser on Lough Derg	..	..	1·50	2·50
639/41		..	*Set of 3*	3·25	4·00

(Des C. Rycraft. Litho Irish Security Stamp Ptg Ltd)

1986 (10 July). *150th Anniv of British and Irish Steam Packet Company.* T **229** *and similar horiz design. Multicoloured.* P 15 × 14.

642	24p. Type **229**	..	..	75	1·00
643	28p. M.V. *Leinster* (modern ferry)	..	..	85	60

230 Kish Lighthouse and Bell 206B Jet Ranger III Helicopter

231 J. P. Nannetti (first president) and Linotype Operator (Dublin Council of Trade Unions Centenary)

(Des R. Ballagh. Litho Irish Security Stamp Printing Ltd)

1986 (10 July). *Irish Lighthouses.* T **230** *and similar vert design. Multicoloured.* P 14 × 15.

644	24p. Type **230**	..	..	75	75
645	30p. Fastnet Lighthouse	..	..	1·75	2·75

(Des R. Ballagh (Nos. 646/7), M. Cameron (No. 648), A. Mazer (Nos. 649/50). Litho Irish Security Stamp Ptg Ltd)

1986 (21 Aug). *Anniversaries and Commemorations.* T **231** *and similar designs. Ordinary paper* (24p.) *or chalk-surfaced paper* (others). P 14 × 15 (*Nos.* 646/7, 649) *or* 15 × 14 (others).

646	24p. multicoloured	..	..	50	90
647	28p. black and brownish grey	..	..	60	80
648	28p. multicoloured	..	..	60	80
649	30p. multicoloured	..	..	65	1·00
650	46p. multicoloured	..	..	70	1·75
646/50		..	*Set of 5*	2·75	4·75

Designs: *Vert*—No. 647, Arthur Griffith (statesman); No. 649, Clasped hands (International Peace Year). *Horiz*—No. 648, Woman surveyor (Women in Society); No. 650, Peace dove (International Peace Year).

232 William Mulready and his Design for 1840 Envelope

233 "The Adoration of the Shepherds" (Francesco Pascucci)

(Des C. Harrison (24p.), A. Mazer from aquatints by M. A. Hayes (others). Litho Irish Security Stamp Ptg Ltd)

1986 (2 Oct). *Birth Bicentenaries of William Mulready* (artist) (24p.) *and Charles Bianconi* (originator of Irish mail coach service) (others). T **232** *and similar multicoloured designs. Chalk-surfaced paper.* P 14 × 15 (28p.) or 15 × 14 (others).

651	24p. Type **232**	..	..	65	70
652	28p. Bianconi car outside Hearns Hotel, Clonmel (*vert*)		..	75	55
653	39p. Bianconi car on the road	..	..	1·25	1·75
651/3	..	..	*Set of 3*	2·40	2·75

(Des C. O'Neill (21p.). Litho Irish Security Stamp Ptg Ltd)

1986 (20 Nov). *Christmas.* T **233** *and similar multicoloured design. Chalk-surfaced paper.* P 15 × 14 (21p.) or 14 × 15 (28p.).

654	21p. Type **233**	..	..	1·10	1·40
	a. Sheetlet. No. 654 × 12	..	..	12·00	
655	28p. "The Adoration of the Magi" (Frans Francken III) (*vert*)		..	65	60

No. 654 was only issued in sheetlets of 12 sold at £2.50, providing a discount of 2p. off the face value of the stamps.

234 "Butterfly and Flowers" (Tara Collins)

235 Cork Electric Tram

(Litho Irish Security Stamp Ptg Ltd)

1987 (27 Jan) *Greetings Stamps. Children's Paintings. T* **234** *and similar multicoloured design. Chalk-surfaced paper. P* 15 × 14 (24p.) *or* 14 × 15 (28p.).

656	24p. Type **234** ..	..	70	1·25
657	28p. "Postman on Bicycle delivering Hearts"			
	(Brigid Teehan) (*vert*)	.. ..	80	1·25

(Des C. Rycraft. Litho Irish Security Stamp Ptg Ltd)

1987 (4 Mar). *Irish Trams. T* **235** *and similar horiz designs. Multicoloured. Chalk-surfaced paper. P* 15 × 14.

658	24p. Type **235**	..	65	65
659	28p. Dublin standard tram No. 291	..	70	85
660	30p. Howth (Great Northern Railway) tram		80	2·00
661	46p. Galway horse tram	.. ..	1·25	2·25
658/61		*Set of* 4	3·00	5·00
MS662	131×85 mm. Nos. 658/61	..	4·25	6·50

No. **MS**662 exists with the sheet margins overprinted in red for "HAFNIA 87" and in black for "STAMPA 87".

236 Ships from Crest (Bicentenary of Waterford Chamber of Commerce)

237 Bord na Mona Headquarters and "The Turf Cutter" sculpture (John Behan), Dublin

(Des K. Uhlemann (24p.), J Farrer (28p.), A. Mazer and Wendy Walsh (30p.), M. Cameron (39p.). Litho Irish Security Stamp Ptg Ltd)

1987 (9 Apr). *Anniversaries. T* **236** *and similar designs. Chalk-surfaced paper. P* 14 × 15 (30p.) *or* 15 × 14 (*others*).

663	24p. black, ultramarine and deep grey-green	80	60
664	28p. multicoloured	.. ..	80	60
665	30p. multicoloured	.. ..	85	1·75
666	39p. multicoloured	.. ..	90	2·00
663/6		*Set of* 4	3·00	4·50

Designs: *Horiz*—28p. Canon John Hayes and symbols of agriculture and development (Birth centenary and 50th anniv of Muintir na Tire Programme); 39p. Mother Mary Martin and International Missionary Training Hospital, Drogheda (50th anniv of Medical Missionaries of Mary). *Vert*—30p. Calceolaria burbidgei and College crest (300th anniv of Trinity College Botanic Gardens, Dublin).

(Des M. Lunt. Litho Harrison)

1987 (14 May). *Europa. Modern Architecture. T* **237** *and similar horiz design. Multicoloured. P* 15 × 14.

667	28p. Type **237** ..	.. ..	1·50	60
668	39p. St. Mary's Church, Cong	.. ..	3·50	5·00

(Des B. Driscoll. Litho Irish Security Stamp Ptg Ltd)

1987 (2 July). *Irish Cattle. T* **238** *and similar horiz designs. Multicoloured. Chalk-surfaced paper. P* 15 × 14.

669	24p. Type **238** ..	.. ..	70	75
670	28p. Friesian cow and calf	..	85	60
671	30p. Hereford bullock	..	90	2·25
672	39p. Shorthorn bull	.. ..	1·00	2·25
669/72		*Set of* 4	3·00	5·25

(Des R. Ballagh. Litho Irish Security Stamp Ptg Ltd)

1987 (27 Aug). *Festivals. T* **239** *and similar multicoloured designs. Chalk-surfaced paper. P* 14 × 15 (*vert*) *or* 15 × 14 (*horiz*).

673	24p. Type **239** ..	..	65	70
674	28p. Rose of Tralee International Festival ..	70	60
675	30p. Wexford Opera Festival (*horiz*)	..	80	2·00
676	46p. Ballinasloe Horse Fair (*horiz*) ..	1·10	2·00
673/6 ..		*Set of* 4	3·00	4·75

240 Flagon (1637), Arms and Anniversary Ornament (1987) (350th Anniv of Dublin Goldsmiths' Company)

241 Scenes from "The Twelve Days of Christmas" (carol)

(Des B. Donegan (No. 677), R. Ballagh (No. 678), A. Mazer and Breda Mathews (No. 679), Libby Carton (No. 680). Litho Harrison (46p.) or Irish Security Stamp Ptg Ltd (*others*))

1987 (1 Oct). *Anniversaries and Commemorations. T* **240** *and similar designs. Ordinary paper* (46p.) *or chalk-surfaced paper* (*others*). *P* 15 × 14 (*horiz*) *or* 14 × 15 (*vert*).

677	**240** 24p. multicoloured	.. ..	55	80
678	– 24p. grey and black	..	55	80
679	– 28p. multicoloured	..	65	60
680	– 46p. multicoloured	..	1·00	1·10
677/80		*Set of* 4	2·50	3·00

Designs: *Vert*—24p. (No. 678) Cathal Brugha (statesman); 46p. Woman chairing board meeting (Women in Society). *Horiz*—28p. Arms of Ireland and inscription (50th anniv of Constitution).

(Des M. Cameron (21p.), A. Mazer (others). Litho Irish Security Stamp Ptg Ltd)

1987 (17 Nov). *Christmas. T* **241** *and similar multicoloured designs. Chalk-surfaced paper. P* 15 × 14 (21p.) *or* 14 × 15 (*others*).

681	21p. Type **241** ..	.. ..	60	1·00
	a. Sheetlet. No. 681 × 14 ..	..	7·50	
682	24p. The Nativity (detail, late 15th-cent Waterford Vestments) (*vert*)	..	75	1·00
683	28p. Figures from Neapolitan crib, *c* 1850 (*vert*)	.. ..	75	80
681/3 ..		*Set of* 3	1·90	2·50

No. 681 represents a special rate for greetings cards within Ireland and to all E.E.C. countries. It was only issued in sheetlets of 14 stamps and 1 label sold at £2.90, providing an additional discount of 4p. off the face value of the stamps.

238 Kerry Cow   **239** Fleadh Nua, Ennis

242 Acrobatic Clowns spelling "LOVE"

243 "Robert Burke" (Sidney Nolan) and Map of Burke and Wills Expedition Route

(Des M. Cameron (24p.), Aislinn Adams (28p.). Litho Irish
Security Stamp Ptg Ltd)

1988 (27 Jan). *Greetings Stamps. T* **242** *and similar multicoloured design. Chalk-surfaced paper. P* 15×14 (24p.) *or*
14×15 (28p.).
684	24p. Type **242**..	.. .. ..	60	60
685	28p. Pillar box and hearts (*vert*)	.. ..	65	65

(Des A. Mazer. Litho Irish Security Stamp Ptg Ltd)

1988 (1 Mar). *Bicentenary of Australian Settlement. T* **243** *and
similar horiz design. Multicoloured. Chalk-surfaced paper.
P* 15×14.
686	24p. Type **243**..	.. ..	40	60
687	46p. "Eureka Stockade" (mural detail, Sidney Nolan)	.. ..	85	1·75

244 Past and Present
Buildings of Dublin

245 Showjumping

(Des S. Conlin. Litho Irish Security Stamp Ptg Ltd)

1988 (1 Mar). *Dublin Millennium. Chalk-surfaced paper.
P* 15×14.
688	**244** 28p. multicoloured	60	55
	a. Booklet pane. No. 688 × 4 ..	..	1·75

No. 688a was printed with either Irish or English inscriptions
in the centre of the pane and came from £2.24 stamp booklets.
Loose panes could also be purchased from the Philatelic Bureau,
Dublin, and its agents. They exist overprinted for "STAMPA 88"
(in blue on Irish version and red on English) and "Sydpex 88"
(both green on gold).

(Des Ann Flynn Litho Irish Security Stamp Ptg Ltd)

1988 (7 Apr). *Olympic Games, Seoul. T* **245** *and similar horiz
design. Multicoloured. Chalk-surfaced paper. P* 15×14.
689	28p. Type **245**	1·00	1·40
	a. Sheetlet. Nos. 689/90, each × 5	..	9·00
690	28p. Cycling	1·00	1·40

Nos. 689/90 were printed together, *se-tenant*, in a sheetlet
containing five of each design and two stamp-size labels.

(Des R. Ballagh (24p.), J. Farrer (30p.), K. Uhlemann (50p.).
Litho Irish Security Stamp Ptg Ltd)

1988 (7 Apr). *Anniversaries and Events. T* **246** *and similar
designs. Chalk-surfaced paper. P* 14×15 (*vert*) *or* 15×14
(*horiz*).
691	24p. brownish grey and black	.. ..	60	45
692	30p. multicoloured	.. ..	1·00	1·00
693	50p. multicoloured	.. ..	1·25	1·90
691/3		*Set of* 3	2·50	3·00

Designs: *Horiz*—30p. Members with casualty and ambulance
(50th anniv of Order of Malta Ambulance Corps). *Vert*—50p.
Barry Fitzgerald (actor) (Birth centenary).

(Des C. Rycraft (28p.), M. Cameron (39p.). Litho Irish
Security Stamp Ptg Ltd)

1988 (12 May). *Europa. Transport and Communications.
T* **247** *and similar horiz design. Multicoloured. Chalk-
surfaced paper. P* 15×14.
694	28p. Type **247**	.. .. ..	1·25	55
695	39p. Globe with stream of letters from Ireland to Europe	.. ..	1·75	2·50

248 *Sirius* (paddle-steamer)
(150th anniv of regular
transatlantic steamship
services)

249 Cottonweed

(Des C. Rycraft. Litho Irish Security Stamp Ptg Ltd)

1988 (12 May). *Transatlantic Transport Anniversaries. T* **248**
*and similar horiz design. Multicoloured. Chalk-surfaced
paper. P* 15×14.
696	24p. Type **248**	75	50
697	46p. Short S.20 seaplane *Mercury* and Short S.21 flying boat *Maia* (Short-Mayo composite aircraft) in Foynes Harbour (50th anniv of first commercial transatlantic flight) ..	1·50	2·75

(Des Frances Poskitt. Litho Irish Security Stamp Ptg Ltd)

1988 (21 June). *Endangered Flora of Ireland. T* **249** *and
similar vert designs. Multicoloured. Chalk-surfaced paper.
P* 14×15.
698	24p. Type **249**	.. .. ..	65	55
699	28p. Hart's Saxifrage	.. ..	75	55
700	46p. Purple Milk-Vetch	.. ..	1·10	2·00
698/700	.. ..	*Set of* 3	2·25	2·75

246 William T.
Cosgrave (statesman)

247 Air Traffic Controllers
and Airbus Industrie A320

250 Garda on Duty

251 Computer and
Abacus (Institute of
Chartered
Accountants in
Ireland Centenary)

Quality Irish Stamps

— *Direct to your Door* —

Buying Stamps by Mail Order?
Make sure you use the
Stanley Gibbons Mail Order Service.

- **SERVICE.** We can offer you a friendly, highly efficient service supported by 143 years of philatelic experience.

- **QUALITY.** The range and depth of our stock is World famous. Most items can be supplied immediately – always of the highest quality and backed by the Stanley Gibbons guarantee of authenticity.

- **QUICK DESPATCH.** We endeavour to send the completed orders out within 48 hours of receiving them.

- **FREE TELEPHONE ADVICE.** We are always happy to discuss your requirements over the telephone and to answer any questions you may have regarding our service or your collection.

- **BUDGET PLANS AND INTEREST FREE** payment schemes available to spread the cost on any purchases over £100.00.

- **PERSONAL SERVICE** from our Mail Order Team dedicated to hand picking your stamps and personally following your order from when it arrives to when it leaves our offices.

- **SPECIALIST "WANTS LIST" SERVICE.** In addition to our mail order stamps, we have an extensive stock of errors, varieties, shades, multiples and postal history. This ensures we can cater for all collectors. "Wants Lists" are most welcome and can be sent by post, fax or e-mail.

- **REGULAR ILLUSTRATED LISTINGS** for many popular countries and themes currently used by thousands of collectors worldwide. They contain our comprehensive range of stamps complete with colour illustrations, accurate descriptions and SG catalogue numbers.
  The one-country listings are now thematic coded to cover 37 different thematic collecting areas.

TURN THE PAGE TO ORDER TODAY

TO ORDER

To order stamps direct from this catalogue, simply detach these centre pages, list the Stanley Gibbons reference number and a brief description. State your preference for 'mint' or 'used' and the price as it appears in this catalogue. Please add postage and packing at £1.50 and calculate the total. (Note: minimum order is £20). Please read the terms and conditions and then complete your personal and payment details on page IV. Send to the address below for our immediate attention.

RETURN TO:
Stanley Gibbons Mail Order,
399 Strand, London, WC2R 0LX
Telephone: (+44) 020 7836 8444
Facsimile: (+44) 020 7836 7342
e-mail: mailorder@stangiblondon.demon.co.uk
Internet: http://www.stangib.com/

BY APPOINTMENT
TO HER MAJESTY
THE QUEEN
STANLEY GIBBONS LTD
LONDON PHILATELISTS

S.G. Ref Number	Description	Mint or Used	Price	Office use only
	Balance to be carried forward		£	

S.G. Ref Number	Description	Mint or Used	Price	Office use only
	Balance from previous page		£	
	Allow £1.50 for postage and packing		£ 1.50	
	Total payable		£	

TERMS AND CONDITIONS

(Please read carefully before ordering)

① **Minimum order £20** (excluding P&P). Minimum stamp price **30p**

② **Please order complete sets only**, we are unable to supply individual stamps from sets.

③ **We can only supply mint (unmounted mint after 1937), and fine used stamps from this catalogue.** First day covers and presentation packs are not available.

④ **Please submit alternatives should your preferred requests be unavailable.** Alternatively you will be sent a credit note for use against you next order, if paying by cheque.

⑤ **All orders will be despatched within 48 hours of receipt of payment.** We cannot accept responsibility for delays caused in the mail.

⑥ **The quality of our stamps is guaranteed**, if you are dissatisfied in any way please return your stamps within 14 days for a full refund.

⑦ **All original order forms are returned with completed orders.**

This does not affect your statutory rights

☐ Please send me a catalogue of your latest publications and accessories.

☐ Please send me your current list of mail order brochures.

☐ Please send me the latest British Europe list containing the stamps of Ireland, Malta, Gibraltar and Cyprus.

CUSTOMER DETAILS

Name (Mr/Mrs/Miss/Ms) _____

Address _____

_____

Postcode _____ Telephone _____

I enclose my cheque/postal order made payable to Stanley Gibbons Ltd for | £ |

I authorise you to charge my   VISA ☐   MasterCard ☐   AMERICAN EXPRESS ☐   ⬤) ☐   ⬔ SWITCH ☐

Card Number ☐☐☐☐☐☐☐☐☐☐☐☐☐☐☐☐☐☐

Expiry Date ☐☐☐   Issue No. or Start Date (Switch Only) ☐☐

Signature _____

At various times, Stanley Gibbons promote a number of products only to their existing customers. If you would prefer not to receive details of these, or of products and services from other reputable companies, please write to: The Data Protection Officer, Stanley Gibbons Publications, 5 Parkside, Christchurch Road, Ringwood, Hampshire, England BH24 3SH

● OUR NAME IS YOUR GUARANTEE OF QUALITY ●

(Des D. Teskey. Litho Irish Security Stamp Ptg Ltd)

1988 (23 Aug). *Irish Security Forces. T 250 and similar horiz designs. Multicoloured. Chalk-surfaced paper. P 15×14.*
701	28p. Type **250**	..	60	1·00
	a. Strip of 4. Nos. 701/4	..	2·25	
702	28p. Army unit with personnel carrier	..	60	1·00
703	28p. Navy and Air Corps members with *Eithne* (helicopter patrol vessel)		60	1·00
704	28p. Army and navy reservists	..	60	1·00
701/4	..	*Set of* 4	2·25	3·50

Nos. 701/4 were printed together, both horizontally and vertically *se-tenant*, throughout the sheet of 20 (4×5).

(Des C. Rycraft (24p.), K. King and A. Mazer (46p.). Litho Irish Security Stamp Ptg Ltd)

1988 (6 Oct). *Anniversaries. T 251 and similar multicoloured design. Chalk-surfaced paper. P 14×15 (24p.) or 15×14 (46p.).*
705	24p. Type **251**	..	40	40
706	46p. *Duquesa Santa Ana* off Donegal (*horiz*) (400th anniv of Spanish Armada)	..	1·25	1·25

252 "President Kennedy" (James Wyeth)

253 St. Kevin's Church, Glendalough

(Des A. Mazer. Litho Irish Security Stamp Ptg Ltd)

1988 (24 Nov). *25th Death Anniv of John F. Kennedy (American statesman). Chalk-surfaced paper. P 15×14.*
707	**252** 28p. multicoloured	..	70	80

(Des Ann Flynn (21p.), B. Donegan (others). Litho Irish Security Stamp Ptg Ltd)

1988 (24 Nov). *Christmas. T 253 and similar vert designs. Multicoloured. Chalk-surfaced paper. P 14×15.*
708	21p. Type **253**	..	70	70
	a. Sheetlet. No. 708 × 14	..	9·00	
709	24p. The Adoration of the Magi	..	50	60
710	28p. The Flight into Egypt	..	60	55
711	46p. The Holy Family	..	70	2·00
708/11	..	*Set of* 4	2·25	3·50

No. 708 represents a special rate for greetings cards within Ireland and to all E.E.C. countries. It was only issued in sheetlets of 14 stamps and 1 label sold at £2.90, providing an additional discount of 4p. off the face value of the stamps.

The designs of Nos. 709/11 are from a 15th-century French Book of Hours.

(Des Susan Dubsky (24p.), A. Mazer (28p.). Litho Irish Security Stamp Ptg Ltd)

1989 (24 Jan). *Greetings Stamps. T 254 and similar multicoloured design. Chalk-surfaced paper. P 15×14 (24p.) or 14×15 (28p.).*
712	24p. Type **254**	..	60	55
713	28p. "The Sonnet" (William Mulready) (*vert*)		65	55

(Des Frances Poskitt. Litho Irish Security Stamp Ptg Ltd)

1989 (11 Apr). *National Parks and Gardens. T 255 and similar horiz designs. Multicoloured. Chalk-surfaced paper. P 15×14.*
714	24p. Type **255**	..	80	55
715	28p. Lough Veagh, Glenveagh National Park	..	95	55
716	32p. Barnaderg Bay, Connemara National Park	..	1·00	1·25
717	50p. St. Stephen's Green, Dublin	..	1·50	1·75
714/17	..	*Set of* 4	3·75	3·75

256 "Silver Stream", 1908   **257** Ring-a-ring-a-roses

(Des C. Rycraft. Litho Irish Security Stamp Ptg Ltd)

1989 (11 Apr). *Classic Irish Cars. T 256 and similar horiz designs. Multicoloured. Chalk-surfaced paper. P 15×14.*
718	24p. Type **256**	..	50	55
	a. Booklet pane. Nos. 718/19, each ×2	..	3·00	
	b. Booklet pane. Nos. 718/21	..	3·50	
719	28p. Benz "Comfortable", 1898	..	50	55
720	39p. "Thomond", 1929	..	1·25	1·50
721	46p. Chambers' 8 h.p. model, 1905	..	1·50	1·60
718/21	..	*Set of* 4	3·25	3·75

Booklet panes Nos. 718a/b come from £2.41 stamp booklets and stamps from them have one or two adjacent sides imperforate. Such panes were also available loose from the Philatelic Bureau, Dublin, and its agents

(Des C. Harrison. Litho Irish Security Stamp Ptg Ltd)

1989 (11 May). *Europa. Children's Games. T 257 and similar horiz design. Multicoloured. Chalk-surfaced paper. P 15×14.*
722	24p. Type **257**	..	1·00	75
723	39p. Hopscotch	..	1·40	2·25

Nos. 722/3 were each issued in sheets of 10 showing additional illustrations in the left-hand sheet margin.

254 Spring Flowers spelling "Love" in Gaelic

255 Italian Garden, Garinish Island

258 Irish Red Cross Flag (50th anniv)

259 Saints Kilian, Totnan and Colman (from 12th-century German manuscript)

(Des Q Design (24p.), R. Hoek (28p.). Litho Irish Security Stamp Ptg Ltd)

1989 (11 May). *Anniversaries and Events. T 258 and similar vert design. Chalk-surfaced paper. P 14×15.*

724	24p. vermilion and black			55	60
725	28p. new blue, black and lemon			1·10	1·10

Design:—28p. Circle of twelve stars (Third direct elections to European Parliament).

(Des P. Effert. Litho Irish Security Stamp Ptg Ltd)

1989 (15 June). *1300th Death Anniv of Saints Kilian, Totnan and Colman. Chalk-surfaced paper. P 13¹/₂.*

726	**259**	28p. multicoloured		80	1·10
		a. Booklet pane. No. 726×4 with			
		margins all round		3·00	

A stamp in a similar design was issued by West Germany. No. 726a exists with text in Irish, English, German or Latin on the pane margin.

260 19th-century Mail Coach passing Cashel

261 Crest and 19th-century Dividers (150th anniv of Royal Institute of Architects of Ireland)

(Des Katie O'Sullivan and B. Donegan. Litho Irish Security Stamp Ptg Ltd)

1989 (27 July). *Bicentenary of Irish Mail Coach Service. Chalk-surfaced paper. P 15×14.*

727	**260**	28p. multicoloured		1·00	75

(Des R. Ballagh (24p.), A. Mazer (28p.), K. Uhlemann (30p.), Carey Clarke (46p.). Litho Irish Security Stamp Ptg Ltd)

1989 (27 July). *Anniversaries and Commemorations. T 261 and similar designs. Chalk-surfaced paper. P 15×14 (30p.) or 14×15 (others).*

728	24p. grey and black			60	55
729	28p. multicoloured			65	55
730	30p. multicoloured			1·40	1·75
731	46p. orange-brown			1·60	1·75
728/31			Set of 4	3·75	4·25

Designs: Vert—24p. Sean T. O'Kelly (statesman) (drawing by Sean Ó'Sullivan); 46p. Jawaharlal Nehru (Birth centenary). Horiz—30p. Margaret Burke-Sheridan (soprano) (portrait by De Gennaro) and scene from *La Bohème* (Birth centenary).

262 *"NCB Ireland* rounding Cape Horn" (Des Fallon)

263 Willow/Red Grouse

(Des I. Caulder. Litho Irish Security Stamp Ptg Ltd)

1989 (31 Aug). *First Irish Entry in Whitbread Round the World Yacht Race. Chalk-surfaced paper. P 15×14.*

732	**262**	28p. multicoloured		1·25	1·25

(Des R. Ward. Litho Irish Security Stamp Ptg Ltd)

1989 (5 Oct). *Game Birds. T 263 and similar square designs. Multicoloured. Chalk-surfaced paper. P 13¹/₂.*

733	24p. Type **263**			1·00	55
734	28p. Lapwing			1·10	55
735	39p. Woodcock			1·40	2·25
736	46p. Ring-necked Pheasant			1·50	2·25
733/6			Set of 4	4·50	5·00
MS737	128×92 mm. Nos. 733/6			4·50	5·00

No. **MS737** exists overprinted on the margins to commemorate "STAMPA 89", the Irish National Stamp Exhibition.

264 "The Annunciation"

265 Logo (Ireland's Presidency of the European Communities)

(Des Jacinta Fitzgerald (21p.), J. McEvoy from 13th-century Flemish Psalter (others). Litho Irish Security Stamp Ptg Ltd)

1989 (14 Nov). *Christmas. T 264 and similar vert designs. Multicoloured. Chalk-surfaced paper. P 14×15.*

738	21p. Children decorating crib			75	75
	a. Sheetlet. No. 738×14			9·50	
739	24p. Type **264**			85	60
740	28p. "The Nativity"			90	55
741	46p. "The Adoration of the Magi"			1·75	2·50
738/41			Set of 4	3·75	4·00

No. **738** represents a special rate for greetings cards within Ireland and to all E.E.C. countries. It was only issued in sheetlets of 14 stamps and 1 label sold at £2.90, providing an additional discount of 4p. off the face value of the stamps.

(Des B. Donegan (30p.), Q Design (50p.). Litho Irish Security Stamp Ptg Ltd)

1990 (9 Jan). *European Events. T 265 and similar horiz design. Multicoloured. Chalk-surfaced paper. P 15×14.*

742	30p. Type **265**			75	60
743	50p. Logo and outline map of Ireland (European Tourism Year)			2·00	3·00

266 Dropping Messages from Balloon

267 Silver Kite Brooch

(Des Aislinn Adams (26p.), Patricia Sleeman and R. Vogel (30p.). Litho Irish Security Stamp Ptg Ltd)

1990 (30 Jan). *Greetings Stamps. T 266 and similar vert design. Chalk-surfaced paper. P 14×15.*

744	26p. multicoloured			1·25	1·25
745	30p. rosine, pale buff and reddish brown			1·25	1·25

Design:—30p. Heart and "Love" drawn in lipstick.

Two Types of 20, 28, 52p.:

A. Irish Security Stamp Ptg Ltd printing (coarse background screen. Less distinct centre detail)

B. Enschedé printing (fine background screen. Clear centre detail)

Two Types of £1, £2, £3:

C. Irish Security Stamp Ptg Ltd printing

D. Enschedé printing

(Des M. Craig and Q Design. Litho Walsall (Nos. 748c, 755b), Enschedé (Nos. 751b, 753b, 762b, 763b, 764b, 765b) or Irish Security Stamp Ptg Ltd (others))

1990 (8 Mar)–97. *Irish Heritage and Treasures.* T **267** *and similar designs. Chalk-surfaced paper* (5, 20, 26, 28, 30, 32, 37, 38, 41, 44, 50, 52p., £1, £5) *or ordinary paper* (*others*). P 14×15 (10, 20, 30, 32p, £5) *or* 15×14 (*others*).

746	1p. black and new blue (26.7.90)	..	10	10
	a. Chalk-surfaced paper (10.91)		30	30
747	2p. black and bright red-orange (26.7.90)		10	10
	a. Chalk-surfaced paper (15.11.90)		10	10
	ab. Booklet pane. Nos. 747a, 748b×3, 752 and 754×2 plus label		3·00	
	ac. Booklet pane Nos. 747a×2, 755×2 and 820 (17.10.91)	..	5·50	
748	4p. black and bluish violet (26.7.90)	..	10	10
	a. Booklet pane. Nos. 748 and 755a×3 (16.11.95)	..	2·00	
	b. Chalk-surfaced paper (15.11.90)		75	1·00
	ba. Booklet pane. Nos. 748b×3, 753×4 plus label (17.10.91)		5·50	
	bb. Booklet pane. Nos. 748b and 1084×3 (6.3.97)	..	1·60	
	c. Perf 13×13¹/₂. Chalk-surfaced paper (24.9.93)	..	10	10
	ca. Booklet pane. Nos. 748c and 755b×3 (4p. at bottom right)		2·00	
	cb. Ditto, but 4p., at top left (2.3.94)	..	2·00	
749	5p. black and bright green (29.1.91)		10	10
	a. Ordinary paper (5.92)	..	1·00	1·00
750	10p. black and bright red-orange (26.7.90)		20	25
	a. Chalk-surfaced paper (9.93)		1·00	1·00
751	20p. black and lemon (A) (29.1.91)	..	35	40
	a. Ordinary paper (3.92)		1·50	1·50
	b. Type B (Enschedé ptg) (16.11.95)		1·00	1·00
752	26p. black and bluish violet	..	45	50
	a. Ordinary paper (5.90)	..	2·50	1·50
	ab. Perf 13¹/₂ (3.5.90)	..	5·00	5·00
753	28p. black & bright red-orange (A) (3.4.91)		50	55
	a. Ordinary paper (5.91)	..	2·00	2·00
	b. Type B (Enschedé ptg) (16.11.95)		1·00	1·00
754	30p. black and new blue	..	55	60
	a. Ordinary paper (5.90)	..	1·50	1·50
	ab. Perf 13¹/₂ (3.5.90)	..	5·00	5·00

755	32p. black and bright green	..	60	65
	a. Ordinary paper (5.90)	..	2·00	2·00
	b. Perf 13¹/₂×13. Chalk-surfaced paper (24.9.93)	..	90	90
756	34p. black and lemon (26.7.90)	..	1·00	1·00
757	37p. brownish black & brt green (3.4.91)		1·25	1·25
	a. Ordinary paper (11.91)	..	3·00	3·50
758	38p. black and bluish violet (3.4.91)		1·25	1·25
	a. Ordinary paper (5.95)	..	3·00	3·00
758b	40p. black and new blue (14.5.92)		1·25	1·25
	ba. Chalk-surfaced paper (9.93)		3·50	3·50
759	41p. black and bright red-orange		70	75
	a. Ordinary paper (10.90)	..	3·25	3·25
760	44p. agate and lemon (3.4.91)	..	75	80
760a	45p. black and bluish violet (14.5.92)		1·25	1·25
761	50p. black and lemon	..	1·25	1·25
	a. Ordinary paper (5.90)	..	3·50	3·50
762	52p. black and new blue (A) (3.4.91)		1·50	1·50
	a. Ordinary paper (2.96)	..	12·00	12·00
	b. Type B (Enschedé ptg) (16.11.95)	..	1·50	1·75
763	£1 black and lemon (C)	..	1·75	1·90
	a. Ordinary paper (5.90)	..	15·00	4·00
	b. Type D (Enschedé ptg) (16.11.95)	..	3·00	3·00
764	£2 black and bright green (C) (26.7.90)		3·50	3·75
	a. Chalk-surfaced paper (9.93)	..	9·00	9·00
	b. Type D (Enschedé ptg) (chalk-surfaced paper) (16.11.95)	..	6·00	6·00
765	£5 black and new blue (C) (29.1.91)		9·00	9·25
	a. Ordinary paper (10.97)	..	30·00	35·00
	b. Type D (Enschedé ptg) (16.11.95)	..	15·00	15·00
746/65	.. ..	*Set of 22*	25·00	26·00

Designs: *Vert* (as T **267**)—1p., 2p. Type **267**; 4p., 5p. Dunamase Food Vessel; 26p., 28p. Lismore Crozier; 34p., 37p., 38p., 40p. Gleninsheen Collar; 41p., 44p., 45p. Silver thistle brooch; 50p., 52p. Broighter Boat. (22×38 *mm*)—£5 St. Patrick's Bell Shrine. *Horiz* (as T **267**)—10p. Derrinboy Armlets; 20p. Gold dress fastener; 30p. Enamelled latchet brooch; 32p. Broighter Collar. (38×22 *mm*)—£1 Ardagh Chalice; £2 Tara Brooch.

Nos. 747a and 748b were initially only available from booklet pane No. 747ab, but were subsequently issued in sheet form during March (4p.) and October (2p.) 1991. Nos. 748c and 755b only occur from booklet panes Nos. 748ca/cb.

With the exception of Nos. 747ac and 748ba each of the listed booklet panes shows either the upper and lower edges (Nos. 748a, 748bb) or the three outer edges of the pane imperforate. Booklet panes Nos. 535ca and 547bb, which include Nos. 752ab and 754ab, and also Nos. 747ac and 748ba each have stamps from the right-hand vertical row imperforate at top, right or at foot depending on the format of the design. The following variations exist:

    2p. Imperf at left (booklet pane No. 747ab)
        Imperf at foot (booklet pane No. 747ac)
    4p. Imperf at left or right (booklet pane No. 747ab)
        Imperf at left (booklet panes Nos. 748a, 748bb)
        Imperf at foot (booklet pane No. 748ba)
        Imperf at foot and left (*p* 13×13¹/₂) (booklet pane No. 748ca)
        Imperf at right (*p* 13×13¹/₂) (booklet pane No. 748cb)
   26p. Imperf at top (*p* 13¹/₂) (booklet pane No. 535ca)
        Imperf at foot and left (booklet pane No. 747ab)
   28p. Imperf at foot (*p* 13¹/₂) (booklet pane No. 748ba)
   30p. Imperf at right (*p* 13¹/₂) (booklet pane No. 547bb)
        Imperf at top or top and right (booklet pane No. 747ab)
   32p. Imperf at right (booklet pane No. 747ac)
        Imperf at top or foot (booklet pane No. 748a)
        Imperf at top, top and right or foot (*p* 13¹/₂×13) (booklet pane No. 748ca)
        Imperf at top and right, foot and right or foot (*p* 13¹/₂×x 13) (booklet pane No. 748cb)

For 4, 28 and 32p. stamps in same designs as Nos. 748, 753 and 755, but printed in photogravure, see Nos. 808/10.

For 32p. value as No. 755, but 27×20 mm and self-adhesive see No. 823.

MINIMUM PRICE

The minimum price quote is 10p which represents a handling charge rather than a basis for valuing common stamps. For further notes about prices see introductory pages.

268 Posy of Flowers

269 Player
heading Ball

(Des M. Cameron. Litho Irish Security Stamp Ptg Ltd)

1990 (22 Mar). *Greetings Stamps. T* **268** *and similar vert designs. Multicoloured. P* 14×15.

766	26p. Type **268**	..	..	2·00	2·50
	a. Booklet pane. Nos. 766/9		..	7·50	
767	26p. Birthday presents	..	..	2·00	2·50
768	30p. Flowers, ribbon and horseshoe		..	2·00	2·50
769	30p. Balloons	..	..	2·00	2·50
766/9	..	..	*Set of* 4	7·50	9·00

Nos. 766/9 come from £1.98 discount stamp booklets.
Booklet pane No. 766a exists with the 26p. values at left or right and the right-hand stamp (either No. 767 or 769) imperforate at right. The booklet pane also contains 8 small greetings labels.

(Des C. Harrison. Litho Irish Security Stamp Ptg Ltd)

1990 (5 Apr). *World Cup Football Championship, Italy. T* **269** *and similar vert design. Multicoloured. Chalk-surfaced paper. P* 14×15.

770	30p. Type **269**	..	..	1·50	2·00
	a. Sheetlet. Nos. 770/1, each × 4		..	11·00	
771	30p. Tackling	..	..	1·50	2·00

Nos. 770/1 were printed together, *se-tenant,* in a sheetlet of 8 stamps and 1 central stamp-size label.

270 Battle of the Boyne, 1690

(Des S. Conlin. Litho Irish Security Stamp Ptg Ltd)

1990 (5 Apr). *300th Anniv of the Williamite Wars* (1*st issue). T* **270** *and similar horiz designs. Multicoloured. Chalk-surfaced paper. P* 13½.

772	30p. Type **270**	..	..	1·00	1·50
	a. Pair. Nos. 772/3	..	..	2·00	3·00
773	30p. Siege of Limerick, 1690	..	..	1·00	1·50

Nos. 772/3 were printed together, *se-tenant,* in horizontal and vertical pairs throughout the sheet.
See also Nos. 806/7.

271 1990 Irish Heritage
30p. Stamp and 1840
Postmark

272 General Post
Office, Dublin

(Des Q Design. Litho Irish Security Stamp Ptg Ltd)

1990 (3 May). *150th Anniv of the Penny Black. T* **271** *and similar horiz design. Multicoloured. Chalk-surfaced paper. P* 15×14.

774	30p. Type **271**	..	..	90	90
	a. Ordinary paper	..	..	1·75	2·50
	ab. Booklet pane. Nos. 774a/5a, each × 2	8·50			
775	50p. Definitive stamps of 1922, 1969, 1982 and 1990	..	..	1·50	2·00
	a. Ordinary paper	..	..	2·50	3·00

Nos. 774a and 775a were only issued in booklets.
In booklet pane No. 774ab one example of each value is imperforate at right.
Booklet pane No. 774ab exists with the margins overprinted in red in connection with "STAMPA 90", the Irish National Stamp Exhibition.
For other booklet panes containing Nos. 774a/5a see Nos. 547ba/bb.

(Des P. Keogh. Litho Irish Security Stamp Ptg Ltd)

1990 (3 May). *Europa. Post Office Buildings. T* **272** *and similar vert design. Multicoloured. P* 14 × 15.

776	30p. Type **272**	..	..	1·00	60
777	41p. Westport Post Office, County Mayo	..	1·40	2·75	

Nos. 776/7 were each printed in sheets of 10 stamps and 2 stamp-size labels.

273 Medical Missionary
giving Injection

274 Narcissus
"Foundling" and
Japanese Gardens,
Tully

(Des I. Calder (26, 50p.), R. Ballagh (30p.). Litho Irish Security Stamp Ptg Ltd)

1990 (21 June). *Anniversaries and Events. T* **273** *and similar designs. P* 15×14 *(horiz)* or 14×15 *(vert).*

778	26p. multicoloured	..	..	90	40
779	30p. black ..	..	..	1·00	2·25
780	50p. multicoloured	..	..	1·50	1·50
778/80	..	..	*Set of* 3	3·00	3·75

Designs: *Vert*—30p. Michael Collins (statesman) (Birth centenary). *Horiz*—50p. Missionaries working at water pump (Irish missionary service).

(Des I. Loe. Litho Irish Security Stamp Ptg Ltd)

1990 (30 Aug). *Garden Flowers. T* **274** *and similar vert designs. Multicoloured. P* 14×15.

781	26p. Type **274**	..	..	70	55
	a. Booklet pane. Nos. 781/2, each × 2	..	4·50		
	b. Booklet pane. Nos. 781/4	..	4·50		
782	30p. *Rosa x hibernica* and Malahide Castle gardens	..	..	85	80
783	41p. *Primula* "Rowallane Rose" and Rowallane garden	..	..	1·75	2·00
784	50p. *Erica erigena* "Irish Dusk" and Palm House, National Botanical Gardens ..	2·00	2·25		
781/4	..	..	*Set of* 4	4·75	5·00

Both booklet panes show the stamps as horizontal rows of four imperforate at top and at right. Stamps from the right of the pane, 30p. on No. 781a, 50p. on No. 781b, are imperforate at top and right with the other values imperforate at top only.
No. 781a exists overprinted in blue for Collectors' Road Shows at Waterford and Galway.

Frama label

Klussendorf label

Amiel Pitney/Bowes label

MACHINE LABELS. For a trial period of three months from 8 October 1990 labels in the above designs, ranging in value from 1p. to £99.99, were available from the head post offices at Dublin (Frama), Limerick (Klussendorf) and Cork (Amiel Pitney/Bowes). The Amiel Pitney/Bowes machine (Cork) was taken out of service on 31 January 1991. The other two machines were withdrawn on 31 May 1991.

275 *Playboy of the Western World* (John Synge)

276 Nativity

(Des R. Ballagh. Litho Irish Security Stamp Ptg Ltd)

1990 (18 Oct). *Irish Theatre. T* **275** *and similar horiz designs. Multicoloured. P* 13½.

785	30p. Type **275**	..	..	1·25	1·75
	a. Horiz strip of 4. Nos. 785/8		..	4·50	
786	30p. *Juno and the Paycock* (Sean O'Casey)		1·25	1·75
787	30p. *The Field* (John Keane)	..	..	1·25	1·75
788	30p. *Waiting for Godot* (Samuel Beckett)	..	1·25	1·75
785/8	..	..	..	*Set of* 4	4·50	6·00

Nos. 785/8 were printed together in sheets of 20 (4×5), producing horizontal *se-tenant* strips of 4 and vertical *se-tenant* pairs of Nos. 785 and 788 or 786/7.

(Des Pamela Leonard (No. 789), B. Cronin (others). Litho Irish Security Stamp Ptg Ltd)

1990 (15 Nov). *Christmas. T* **276** *and similar vert designs. Multicoloured. Chalk-surfaced paper* (50p.) *or ordinary paper* (*others*). *P* 14×15.

789	26p. Child praying by bed	..	..	70	80
	a. Sheetlet. No. 789×12		..	7·50	
790	26p. Type **276**	..	..	70	60
791	30p. Madonna and Child	..	..	90	90
792	50p. Adoration of the Magi	..	..	1·60	2·25
789/92	..	..	..	*Set of* 4	3·50	4·00

No. 789 was only issued in sheetlets of 12 sold at £2.86, providing a discount of 26p. off the face value of the stamps.

NEW INFORMATION

The editor is always interested to correspond with people who have new information that will improve or correct the Catalogue.

ÉIRE 26

277 Hearts in Mail Sack and Postman's Cap

The Starley Rover

278 Starley "Rover" Bicycle, 1886

(Des Liz Manning (26p.), Louise Mullally (30p.). Litho Irish Security Stamp Ptg Ltd)

1991 (29 Jan). *Greetings Stamps. T* **277** *and similar vert design. Multicoloured. Chalk-surfaced paper. P* 14×15.

793	26p. Type **277**	..	..	85	1·00
794	30p. Boy and girl kissing	..	..	90	1·00

(Des E. Patton. Litho Irish Security Stamp Ptg Ltd)

1991 (5 Mar). *Early Bicycles. T* **278** *and similar vert designs. Multicoloured. Chalk-surfaced paper. P* 14×15.

795	26p. Type **278**	..	..	80	60
796	30p. Child's horse tricycle, 1875	..	..	90	1·00
797	50p. "Penny Farthing", 1871	..	..	1·60	2·00
795/7	..	..	..	*Set of* 3	3·00	3·25
MS798	113×72 mm. Nos. 795/7	..	..	3·00	3·25

No. **MS**798 exists with privately-applied marginal overprints for the "Collectorex 91" Exhibition, Dublin, the I.P.T.A. Collectors' Road Show, Birr (both in black) and "STAMPA 91" Exhibition, Dublin (in red or blue).

279 Cuchulainn (statue by Oliver Sheppard) and Proclamation

280 Scene from *La Traviata* (50th anniv of Dublin Grand Opera Society)

(Des I. Calder. Litho Irish Security Stamp Ptg Ltd)

1991 (3 Apr). *75th Anniv of Easter Rising. Chalk-surfaced paper. P* 15×14.

799	**279** 32p. multicoloured	..	..	1·25	1·40

(Des K. Uhlemann (28p.), M. Craig and I. Calder (32p.), M. Craig (44p.), M. Craig and Q Design (52p.). Litho Irish Security Stamp Ptg Ltd)

1991 (11 Apr). *"Dublin 1991 European City of Culture". T* **280** *and similar horiz designs. Multicoloured. Chalk-surfaced paper. P* 13½ (52p.) *or* 15×14 (*others*).

800	28p. Type **280**	..	..	65	80
	a. Booklet pane. Nos. 800/2	..	3·75	
	b. Booklet pane. Nos. 800/3	..	3·75	
801	32p. City Hall and European Community emblem	..	85	1·50
802	44p. St. Patrick's Cathedral (800th anniv)	..	90	1·60
803	52p. Custom House (bicent) (41×24 *mm*)	..	1·00	1·60
800/3	..	..	..	*Set of* 4	3·00	5·00

281 *Giotto* Spacecraft
approaching Halley's Comet

(Des C. Rycraft. Litho Irish Security Stamp Ptg Ltd)

1991 (14 May). *Europa. Europe in Space. T* **281** *and similar horiz design. Multicoloured. P* 15×14.
804   32p. Type **281** .. .. 1·25 1·00
805   44p. Hubble Telescope orbiting Earth .. 1·75 3·00
Nos. 804/5 were each issued in sheetlets of 10 (2×5) with illustrations of space launches on enlarged left hand margins.

282 Siege of Athlone

283 John A. Costello
(statesman)

(Des S. Conlin. Litho Irish Security Stamp Ptg Ltd)

1991 (14 May). *300th Anniv of the Williamite Wars (2nd issue). T* **282** *and similar horiz design. Multicoloured. Chalk-surfaced paper. P* 15×14.
806   28p. Type **282** .. .. .. 90 1·40
  a. Pair. Nos. 806/7 .. .. 1·75 2·75
807   28p. Generals Ginkel and Sarsfield (signatories of Treaty of Limerick) .. 90 1·40
Nos. 806/7 were printed together, *se-tenant,* in horizontal and vertical pairs throughout the sheet.

1991 (14 May). *As Nos.* 748, 753 *and* 755, *but printed in photogravure by Enschedé. Chalk-surfaced paper. P* 14×15 (32p.) *or* 15×14 (*others*).
808   4p. black and bluish violet 10 10
  a. Booklet pane. Nos. 808×2, 809 and 810×2 plus label .. .. 2·00
809   28p. black and reddish orange 55 60
810   32p. black and bright green 55 70
808/10 .. .. *Set of 3* 1·25 1·40
Nos. 808/10 were only available in £1 stamp booklets. Booklet pane No. 808a has imperforate outer edges giving stamps imperforate at left or right (4p.), at left and foot (28p.) and at top and right (32p.).

(Des R. Ballagh (28p.), Q Design (others). Litho Irish Security Stamp Ptg, Ltd)

1991 (2 July). *Anniversaries. T* **283** *and similar designs. Chalk-surfaced paper* (28p.). *P* 15×14 (52p.) *or* 14×15 (*others*).
811   28p. black 70 70
812   32p. multicoloured .. .. .. 85 1·00
813   52p. multicoloured .. .. .. 1·40 2·50
811/13 .. .. *Set of 3* 2·75 3·75
Designs: *Vert*—28p. Type **283** (Birth centenary) (drawing by Sean O'Sullivan); 32p. "Charles Stewart Parnell" (Sydney Hall) (Death centenary). *Horiz*—52p. Meeting of United Irishmen (Bicentary).

284 Player on 15th Green,   285 Wicklow
Portmarnock (Walker Cup)   Cheviot

(Des E. Patton. Litho Irish Security Stamp Ptg Ltd)

1991 (3 Sept). *Golf Commemorations. T* **284** *and similar multicoloured design. Chalk-surfaced paper* (32p.). *P* 15×14 (28p.) *or* 14×15 (32p.).
814   28p. Type **284** .. .. .. 1·00 75
815   32p. Logo and golfer of 1900 (Centenary of Golfing Union of Ireland) (*vert*) .. 1·25 1·00

(Des Pamela Leonard. Litho Irish Security Stamp Ptg Ltd)

1991 (3 Sept). *Irish Sheep. T* **285** *and similar multicoloured designs. Chalk-surfaced paper. P* 15×14 (52p.) *or* 14×15 (*others*).
816   32p. Type **285** .. .. .. 1·00 80
817   38p. Donegal Blackface .. .. 1·40 1·75
818   52p. Galway (*horiz*) .. .. 2·00 3·50
816/18 .. .. *Set of 3* 4·00 5·50

286 Boatyard   287 The
                       Annunciation

(Des C. Rycraft. Litho Irish Security Stamp Ptg Ltd)

1991 (17 Oct). *Fishing Fleet. T* **286** *and similar horiz designs. Multicoloured. Chalk-surfaced paper. P* 15×14.
819   28p. Type **286** 60 65
  a. Booklet pane. Nos. 819/22 .. 5·50
  b. Booklet pane. Nos. 819/20 each × 2 .. 5·50
820   32p. Traditional inshore trawlers .. 70 80
821   44p. Inshore lobster pot boat .. 1·60 2·25
822   52p. *Veronica* (fish factory ship) .. 2·00 2·50
819/22 .. .. *Set of 4* 4·00 5·50
In booklet pane No. 819a the 32p. and 52p. values are imperforate at right.
Booklet pane No. 819a exists with the gutter margin overprinted in connection with the "PHILANIPPON '91" International Stamp Exhibition, Tokyo.
For a further booklet pane including No. 820 see No. 747ac.

(Litho Printset-Cambec Pty Ltd, Australia (No. 823) or Irish Security Stamp Ptg Ltd (No. 823a))

1991 (31 Oct)–**95**. *As No.* 755, *but larger,* 27×21 *mm, and self-adhesive. P* 11½.
823   32p. black and bright green 65 70
  a. Perf 10×9 (8.6.95) 65 80
Examples of No. 823 have rounded perforations at each corner of the stamp and pointed die-cut "teeth". No. 823a shows a perforation at each corner and has rounded teeth. Initially both printers showed the stamps separate on the backing paper, but from September 1996 printings of No. 823a retained the surplus self-adhesive paper around each stamp. Printings from July 1992 contained "reminder" labels inserted 20 stamps and 10 stamps from the end of the coil.
Nos. 823/a were only available in coils of 100, or as strips of 3 from the Philatelic Bureau.

(Des Q. Design (No. 827), T. Gayer (others). Litho Irish Security Stamp Ptg Ltd)

1991 (14 Nov). *Christmas. T* **287** *and similar vert designs. Chalk-surfaced paper. P* 14×15.

827	28p. multicoloured	..	..	..	80	85
	a. Sheetlet. No. 827×13..			..	10·00	
828	28p. dull ultramarine, sage-green and black				75	65
829	32p. scarlet and black		..	..	85	75
830	52p. multicoloured		..	..	1·60	2·50
827/30	..	..	..	*Set of* 4	3·50	4·25

Designs:—No. 827, Three Kings; No. 828, Type **287**; No. 829, The Nativity; No. 830, Adoration of the Kings.

No. 827 was only issued in sheetlets of 13 stamps and two labels (at the centre of rows 1 and 2) sold at £3.36 providing a discount of 28p. off the face value of the stamps.

288 Multicoloured Heart

289 Healthy Family on Apple

(Des T. Monaghan (28p.), R. Ballagh (32p.). Litho Irish Security Stamp Ptg Ltd)

1992 (28 Jan). *Greetings Stamps. T* **288** *and similar multicoloured design. P* 15×14 (28p.) *or* 14×15 (32p.).

831	28p. Type **288**	..	..	85	95
832	32p. "LOVE" at end of rainbow (*vert*)	..	95	1·10

(Des Pamela Leonard. Litho Irish Security Stamp Ptg Ltd)

1992 (25 Feb). *"Healthy Living" Campaign. P* 14×15.

833	**289**	28p. multicoloured	..	85	85

290 Boxing

(Des C. Harrison. Litho Irish Security Stamp Ptg Ltd)

1992 (25 Feb). *Olympic Games, Barcelona. T* **290** *and similar horiz design. P* 15×14.

834	32p. Type **290**	..	..	..	90	90
835	44p. Sailing			..	1·40	2·25
MS836	130×85 mm. Nos. 834/5×2		..	4·50	5·00
	a. On chalk-surfaced paper			..	£170	

No. **MS**836 exists overprinted in black on the margin in connection with the "World Columbian Stamp Expo '92", Chicago. The chalk-surfaced paper variety is only known with this marginal overprint.

291 *Mari* (cog) and 14th-century Map

(Des C. Rycraft. Litho Irish Security Stamp Ptg Ltd)

1992 (2 Apr). *Irish Maritime Heritage. T* **291** *and similar multicoloured design. Chalk-surfaced paper. P* 15×14 (32p) *or* 14×15 (52p).

837	32p. Type **291**	..	..	..	1·00	90
838	52p. *Ovoca* (trawler) and chart (*vert*)	..	1·50	2·75

292 Chamber Logo and Commercial Symbols

293 Cliffs and Cove

(Des E. Patton. Litho Irish Security Stamp Ptg Ltd)

1992 (2 Apr). *Bicentenary of Galway Chamber of Commerce and Industry. Chalk-surfaced paper. P* 15×14.

839	**292**	28p. multicoloured	..	..	70	85

(Des Pamela Leonard. Litho Irish Security Stamp Ptg Ltd)

1992 (2 Apr). *Greetings Stamps. T* **293** *and similar vert designs. Multicoloured. Chalk-surfaced paper. P* 14×15.

840	28p. Type **293**	..	..	75	1·10
	a. Booklet pane. Nos. 840/3	..	..	2·75	
841	28p. Meadow		..	75	1·10
842	32p. Fuchsia and Honeysuckle	..	75	1·10
843	32p. Lily pond and dragonfly	..	75	1·10
840/3	..	..	..	*Set of* 4	2·75	4·00

Nos. 840/3 come from £2.40 stamp booklets.

Booklet pane No. 840a exists with the 28p. values at left or right and has the right-hand stamp (either No. 841 or 843) imperforate at right. The booklet pane also contains 8 small greetings labels.

Booklet pane No. 840a exists overprinted on the margin for Regional Stamp Shows at Sligo and Waterford.

MACHINE LABELS. Frama labels in the above design, providing values from 1p. to £99.99, were introduced at head post offices in Dublin (001), Cork (003), Limerick (004) and Galway (005) on 6 April 1992. The system was extended to Bray (008), Killarney (009) and Sligo (007) on 20 July 1992, and to Kilkenny (010) and Waterford (006) on 7 September when a second machine (002) was also provided at Dublin. Both the Dublin machines were relocated to Dublin Airport in August 1994.

294 Fleet of Columbus

(Des S. Conlin. Litho Irish Security Stamp Ptg Ltd)

1992 (14 May). *Europa. 500th Anniv of Discovery of America by Columbus. T* **294** *and similar horiz design. Multicoloured.* *P* 15×14.
844   32p. Type **294** .. .. 1·25   90
845   44p. Columbus landing in the New World   1·75   2·50
   Nos. 844/5 were each issued in sheetlets of 10 (2×5) with illustrated left or right margins.

295 Irish Immigrants

(Des Pamela Leonard. Litho Irish Security Stamp Ptg Ltd)

1992 (14 May). *Irish Immigrants in the Americas. T* **295** *and similar horiz design. Multicoloured. P* 13½.
846   52p. Type **295** .. .. .. 1·60   1·75
   a. Pair. Nos. 846/7 .. .. 3·00   3·50
847   52p. Irish soldiers, entertainers and politicians .. .. .. 1·60   1·75
   Nos. 846/7 were printed together, *se-tenant,* in horizontal and vertical pairs throughout the sheet.

296 Pair of Pine Martens

(Des R. Ward. Litho Irish Security Stamp Ptg Ltd)

1992 (9 July). *Endangered Species. Pine Marten. T* **296** *and similar horiz designs. Multicoloured. P* 15×14.
848   28p. Type **296** .. .. .. 1·00   70
849   32p. Marten on branch .. .. 1·00   80
850   44p. Female with kittens .. .. 1·60   1·50
851   52p. Marten catching Great Tit .. 2·00   1·75
848/51 .. .. *Set of* 4   5·00   4·25

297 "The Rotunda and New Rooms" (James Malton)

(Des J. McEvoy (28, 44p.), E. Patton (32, 52p.). Litho Irish Security Stamp Ptg Ltd)

1992 (2 Sept). *Dublin Anniversaries. T* **297** *and similar multicoloured designs. Chalk-surfaced paper* (32p.). *P* 15×14 (28, 44p.) *or* 13½ (32, 52p.).
852   28p. Type **297** 70   65
853   32p. Trinity College Library (28×45 *mm*)   1·00   1·00
854   44p. "Charlemont House" .. .. 1·10   2·00
855   52p. Trinity College main gate (28×45 *mm*)   1·40   2·25
852/5 .. .. *Set of* 4   3·75   5·50
   Anniversaries:—28, 44p. Bicentenary of publication of Malton's "Views of Dublin"; 32, 52p. 400th anniv of founding of Trinity College.

298 European Star and Megalithic Dolmen   **299** Farm Produce

(Des R. Ballagh. Litho Irish Security Stamp Ptg Ltd)

1992 (15 Oct). *Single European Market. P* 15×14.
856 **298** 32p. multicoloured 70   80
   a. Booklet pane. No. 856×4 .. 3·00
   b. Booklet pane. No. 856×3 .. 3·00
   Three versions of booklet pane No. 856a exist showing the stamps arranged as a block of 4, as singles or in two vertical pairs. The first two versions exist overprinted for "STAMPA '92" (in blue on the block of four pane and in red on the other).
   The booklet panes also exist overprinted for Regional Stamp Shows at Galway, Dundalk, Kilkenny and Limerick.

(Des. Frances Poskitt. Litho Irish Security Stamp Ptg Ltd)

1992 (15 Oct). *Irish Agriculture. T* **299** *and similar vert designs. Multicoloured. P* 14×15.
857   32p. Type **299** .. .. .. 1·00   1·25
   a. Horiz strip of 4. Nos. 857/60 .. 3·50
858   32p. Dairy and beef herds .. .. 1·00   1·25
859   32p. Harvesting cereals .. .. 1·00   1·25
860   32p. Market gardening .. .. 1·00   1·25
857/60 .. .. .. *Set of* 4   3·50   4·50
   Nos. 857/60 were printed together, *se-tenant,* in horizontal strips of 4 throughout the sheet with each strip forming a composite design.

300 "The Annunciation" (from illuminated manuscript)   **301** Queen of Hearts

(Des Frances Poskitt (No. 861), J. McEvoy (others). Litho Irish Security Stamp Ptg Ltd)

1992 (19 Nov). *Christmas. T* **300** *and similar vert designs. Multicoloured. Chalk-surfaced paper. P* 14×15.
861   28p. Congregation entering church .. 80   65
   a. Sheetlet. No. 861×13 .. 9·00
862   32p. Type **300** 80   65
863   32p. "Adoration of the Shepherds" (Da Empoli) .. .. .. 1·10   1·00
864   52p. "Adoration of the Magi" (Rottenhammer) .. .. .. 1·40   1·50
861/4 .. .. .. *Set of* 4   3·75   3·50
   No. 861 was only issued in sheetlets of 13 stamps and two labels (at the centre of rows 1 and 2) sold at £3.36 providing a discount of 28p. off the face value of the stamps.

(Des C. Harrison (28p.), Q. Design (32p.) Litho Irish Security Stamp Ptg Ltd)

1993 (26 Jan). *Greetings Stamps. T* **301** *and similar multicoloured design. Chalk-surfaced paper. P* 14×15 (28p.) *or* 15×14 (32p.).
865   28p. Type **301** 75   75
866   32p. Hot air balloon trailing hearts (*horiz*)   85   85

302 "Evening at Tangier" (Sir John Lavery)

(Des. E. Patton. Litho Irish Security Stamp Ptg Ltd)

1993 (4 Mar). *Irish Impressionist Painters. T* **302** *and similar multicoloured designs. Chalk-surfaced paper. P* 13.
867   28p. Type **302**   75   60
    a. Booklet pane. Nos. 867/70 with
    margins all round   ..   ..   ..   5·00
    b. Booklet pane. Nos. 867/8 with margins
    all round   ..   ..   2·75
868   32p. "The Goose Girl" (William Leech)   80   65
869   44p. "La Jeune Bretonne" (Roderic O'Conor)
    (*vert*) ..   ..   1·25   1·60
    a. Booklet pane. Nos. 869/70 with
    margins all round   ..   ..   ..   2·75
870   52p. "Lustre Jug" (Walter Osborne) (*vert*)   1·75   2·25
867/70   ..   ..   *Set of* 4   4·00   4·50
Booklet pane No. 867a exists in two slightly different versions, one containing two *se-tenant* pairs and the other the stamps perforated individually.

The booklet panes exist overprinted in the margin in connection with Regional Stamp Shows at Mullingar, Tralee (overprint reads "Summer Regional Show"), Cork and Letterkenny. No. 867b also comes with a blue marginal overprint for "STAMPA 93".

303 Bee Orchid

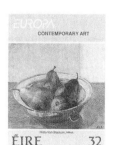

304 "Pears in a Copper Pan" (Hilda van Stockum)

(Des I. Loe. Litho Irish Security Stamp Ptg Ltd)

1993 (20 Apr). *Irish Orchids. T* **303** *and similar vert designs. Multicoloured. P* 14×15.
871   28p. Type **303**   90   60
872   32p. O'Kelly's Orchid   ..   ..   ..   1·00   80
873   38p. Dark Red Helleborine   ..   ..   1·60   2·25
874   52p. Irish Lady's Tresses ..   ..   ..   1·90   2·75
871/4   ..   ..   *Set of* 4   4·75   5·75
MS875   130×71 mm. Nos. 871/4   ..   ..   4·75   6·00
No. **MS**875 exists overprinted in red on the margin in connection with "STAMPA 93". This miniature sheet was also re-issued with a wider upper margin, showing the Irish and Thai flags, for the "Bangkok '93" International Stamp Exhibition. Such sheets were only available from the Philatelic Bureau and the An Post stand at the exhibition.

(Des E. Patton. Litho Irish Security Stamp Ptg Ltd)

1993 (18 May). *Europa. Contemporary Art. T* **304** *and similar vert design. Multicoloured. Chalk-surfaced paper. P* 13.
876   32p. Type **304**   75   75
877   44p. "Arrieta Orzola" (Tony O'Malley)   ..   1·10   1·10
Nos. 876/7 were each issued in sheetlets of 10 stamps and two labels (in positions 1 and 4 of the top row).

305 Cultural Activities

(Des K. Uhlemann and B. Donegan. Litho Irish Security Stamp Ptg Ltd)

1993 (8 July). *Centenary of Conradh Na Gaelige* (*cultural organization*). *T* **305** *and similar multicoloured design. Chalk-surfaced paper. P* 15×14 (32p.) *or* 14×15 (52p.).
878   32p. Type **305**   85   75
879   52p. Illuminated manuscript cover (*vert*) ..   1·50   1·50

306 Diving

(Des C. Harrison. Litho Irish Security Stamp Ptg Ltd)

1993 (8 July). *Centenary of Irish Amateur Swimming Association. T* **306** *and similar horiz design. Multicoloured. Chalk-surfaced paper. P* 15×14.
880   32p. Type **306**   ..   ..   1·00   1·25
    a. Horiz pair. Nos. 880/1   ..   ..   2·00   2·50
881   32p. Swimming   ..   ..   1·00   1·25
Nos. 880/1 were printed together, *se-tenant*, in horizontal pairs throughout the sheet.

307 Nurse with Patient and Hospital Buildings (250th anniv of Royal Hospital, Donnybrook)

(Des K. Uhlemann (28p.), Q Design (32p.), C. Rycraft (44p.), P. Monahan (52p.). Litho Irish Security Stamp Ptg Ltd)

1993 (2 Sept). *Anniversaries and Events. T* **307** *and similar multicoloured designs. Chalk-surfaced paper. P* 15×14 (28p., 44p.), 14×15 (32p.) *or* 13½ (52p.).
882   28p. Type **307**   80   60
883   32p. College building and crest (Bicent of St.
    Patrick's College, Carlow) (*vert*)   ..   80   65
884   44p. Map of Neolithic field system, Céide
    (Opening of interpretative centre)   ..   1·25   1·40
885   52p. Edward Bunting (musicologist) (150th
    death anniv) (25×42 *mm*)   ..   ..   1·40   1·60
882/5   ..   ..   *Set of* 4   3·75   3·75

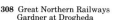

308 Great Northern Railways Gardner at Drogheda

309 The Annunciation

(Des C. Rycraft. Litho Irish Security Stamp Ptg Ltd)

1993 (12 Oct). *Irish Buses. T* **308** *and similar horiz designs.*
Multicoloured. Chalk-surfaced paper. P 15×14.
886	28p. Type **308**	60	65
	a. Booklet pane. Nos. 886/7, each × 2 ..	3·25	
	b. Booklet pane. Nos. 886/9	3·25	
887	32p. C.I.E. Leyland Titan at College Green, Dublin	65	70
888	52p. Horse-drawn omnibus at Old Baal's Bridge, Limerick	1·25	1·90
	a. Horiz pair. Nos. 888/9	2·50	3·75
889	52p. Char-a-banc at Lady's View, Killarney	1·25	1·90
886/9	*Set of* 4	3·25	4·50

Nos. 888/9 were printed together, *se-tenant,* in horizontal
pairs throughout the sheet.

Booklet panes Nos. 886a/b come from £2.84 stamp booklets
and have the outer edges of the pane imperforate.

(Des Pamela Leonard (No. 890), C. Harrison (others). Litho Irish
Security Stamp Ptg Ltd)

1993 (16 Nov). *Christmas. T* **309** *and similar multicoloured*
designs. Chalk-surfaced paper. P 14×15 (*No.* 890) *or* 15×14
(*others*).
890	28p. The Flight into Egypt (*vert*)	60	65
	a. Sheetlet. No. 890×13	5·75	
891	28p. Type **309**	60	55
892	32p. Holy Family	70	70
893	52p. Adoration of the shepherds	1·60	2·25
890/3	*Set of* 4	3·25	3·75

No. 890 was only issued in sheetlets of 13 stamps and two
labels (at the centre of rows 1 and 2) sold at £3.36 providing a
discount of 28p. off the face value of the stamps.

310 Airplane skywriting
"Love"

311 Smiling Sun

(Des Jean Colton (28p.), E. Rainsberry (32p.) Litho Questa)

1994 (27 Jan). *Greetings Stamps. · T* **310** *and similar*
multicoloured design. Chalk-surfaced paper. P 15×14 (28p.)
or 14×15 (32p.).
894	28p. Type **310**	75	75
895	32p. Couple within heart (*vert*)	85	85

(Des S. Young. Litho Irish Security Stamp Ptg)

1994 (27 Jan). *Greetings Booklet Stamps. T* **311** *and similar*
vert designs. Multicoloured. P 14×15.
896	32p. Type **311**	70	85
	a. Booklet pane. No. 896/9	2·50	
897	32p. Smiling daisy	70	85
898	32p. Smiling heart	70	85
899	32p. Smiling rose ..	70	85
896/9	*Set of* 4	2·50	3·00

Nos. 896/9 come from £2.56 stamp booklets.

Booklet pane No. 896a exists with the right-hand stamp
(either No. 897 or 899) imperforate at right. Each booklet pane
also contains 8 small greeting labels.

The booklet pane also exists overprinted for Regional Stamp
Shows at Cork and Letterkenny and from the Dublin
International Stamp and Card Show.

(Des S. Young. Litho Irish Security Stamp Ptg Ltd)

1994 (18 Feb). *"Hong Kong '94" International Stamp*
Exhibition. Chinese New Year ("Year of the Dog"). P 14×15.
MS900 137×34 mm. Nos. 896/8   ..   ..   4·25   4·75
The example of No. 898 in the above miniature sheet is
imperforate at right.

312 Stylised Logo of Macra
na Feirme (50th anniv)

(Des K. and R. Uhlemann (28p.), Creative Inputs (32p.),
E. Patton (38, 52p.). Litho Irish Security Stamp Ptg Ltd)

1994 (2 Mar). *Anniversaries and Events. T* **312** *and similar*
horiz designs. Chalk-surfaced paper. P 15×14.
901	28p. gold and deep ultramarine	75	65
902	32p. multicoloured	1·25	75
903	38p. multicoloured	1·25	1·75
904	52p. black, cobalt and bright blue	1·40	2·00
901/4	*Set of* 4	4·25	4·75

Designs: (38×35 *mm*)—32p. "The Taking of Christ"
(Caravaggio) (Loan of painting to National Gallery). (37½×27
mm)—38p. Sir Horace Plunkett with 19th-century milk carts
and modern tankers (Centenary of Irish Co-operative
Organisation Society); 52p. Congress emblem (Centenary of
Irish Congress of Trade Unions).

313 St. Brendan visiting
Iceland

(Des C. Harrison. Litho Irish Security Stamp Ptg, Ltd)

1994 (18 Apr). *Europa. St. Brendan's Voyages. T* **313** *and*
similar horiz design. Multicoloured. Chalk-surfaced paper.
P 15×14.
905	32p. Type **313**	75	70
906	44p. St. Brendan discovering Faroe Islands	1·50	2·00
MS907	82×76 mm. Nos. 905/6	2·25	2·75

Nos. 905/6 were each issued in sheetlets of 10 (2×5) with
enlarged illustrated left margins.

No. MS907 also exists overprinted in blue on the margins in
connection with "Stampa '94".

314 First Meeting of Dail,
1919

315 Irish and
Argentine Footballers

(Des R. Hoek. Litho Irish Security Stamp Ptg Ltd)

1994 (27 Apr). *Parliamentary Anniversaries. T* **314** *and*
similar horiz design. Multicoloured. Chalk-surfaced paper.
P 15×14.
908	32p. Type **314** (75th anniv)	90	1·00
	a. Booklet pane. Nos. 908/9, each × 2	3·00	
	b. Booklet pane. Nos. 908/9	1·50	
909	32p. European Parliament (4th direct elections)	90	1·00

Booklet panes Nos. 908a/b come from £1.92 stamp booklets
and have the outer edges of the panes imperforate. Booklet pane

No. 908a contains examples of No. 908 either imperforate at top or at right and foot, and No. 909 imperforate at foot or at top and right. In booklet pane No. 908b No. 908 is imperforate at right and No. 909 fully perforated.

(Des J. Donohoe (Nos. 910/11), E. Patton (others). Litho Irish Security Stamp Ptg, Ltd (Nos. 910/11) or Enschedé (others))

1994 (31 May). *Sporting Anniversaries and Events.* T **315** *and similar multicoloured designs. Chalk-surfaced paper (Nos. 910/11).* P 14×15 *(Nos. 910/11) or* 13×13½ *(others).*

910	32p. Type **315**		80	1·00
	a. Sheetlet. Nos. 910/11, each × 4		6·00	
911	32p. Irish and German footballers		80	1·00
912	32p. Irish and Dutch women's hockey match (*horiz*)		1·25	1·00
913	52p. Irish and English women's hockey match (*horiz*)		1·50	2·00
910/13		*Set of 4*	4·00	4·50

Anniversaries and Events:—Nos. 910/11, World Cup Football Championship, U.S.A.; No. 912, Women's Hockey World Cup, Dublin; No. 913, Centenary of Irish Ladies' Hockey Union.

Nos. 910/11 were printed together, *se-tenant*, in sheetlets of 8 stamps and one central label.

316 *Arctia caja*

317 Statue of Edmund Rice and Class

(Des I. Loe)

1994 (12 July). *Moths.* T **316** *and similar horiz designs. Multicoloured.* (a) *Litho Irish Security Stamp Ptg Ltd. Chalk-surfaced paper.* P 15×14.

914	28p. Type **316**		65	60
915	32p. *Calamia tridens*		75	70
916	38p. *Saturnia pavonia*		90	1·10
917	52p. *Deilephila elpenor*		1·50	2·00
914/17		*Set of 4*	3·50	4·00
MS918	120×71 mm. Nos. 914/17		3·50	

(b) *Litho Printset-Cambec Pty Ltd, Australia. Self-adhesive. Chalk-surfaced paper.* P 11½

919	32p. *Calamia tridens*		85	1·10
920	32p. Type **316**		85	1·10
921	32p. *Deilephila elpenor*		85	1·10
922	32p. *Saturnia pavonia*		85	1·10
919/22		*Set of 4*	3·00	4·00

No. **MS**918 also exists with the "Philakorea '94" International Stamp Exhibition, Seoul, logo added at bottom right and also comes overprinted in black for Collectors' Road Show, Sligo, or in red for "Stampa '94".

Nos. 919/22 are smaller, 34×22 mm, and occur, *se-tenant*, in strips of 4 or rolls of 100 with the surplus self-adhesive paper around each stamp removed.

(Des S. Conlin (No. 923), Design Factory (Nos. 925, 927), E. Patton (Nos. 924, 926). Litho Walsall (Nos. 925, 927), Irish Security Stamp Ptg Ltd (others))

1994 (6 Sept). *Anniversaries and Events.* T **317** *and similar multicoloured designs. Chalk-surfaced paper.* P 13½ (No. 923), 14 (Nos. 925, 927), 14×15 (Nos. 924) *or* 15×14 (No. 926).

923	28p. St. Laurence Gate, Drogheda (41½×25 mm)		70	80
924	32p. Type **317**		75	1·10
925	32p. Edmund Burke (politician)		75	1·10
926	52p. Vickers FB-27 Vimy and map (*horiz*)		1·25	1·40
927	52p. Eamonn Andrews (broadcaster)		1·50	1·50
923/7		*Set of 5*	4·50	5·50

Anniversaries and Events:—No. 923, 800th anniv of Drogheda; No. 924, 150th death anniv of Edmund Rice (founder of Irish Christian Brothers); Nos. 925, 927, The Irish abroad; No. 926, 75th anniv of Alcock and Brown's first Transatlantic flight.

318 George Bernard Shaw (author) and *Pygmalion* Poster

319 The Annunciation (ivory plaque)

(Des R. Ballagh. Litho Irish Security Stamp Ptg Ltd)

1994 (18 Oct). *Irish Nobel Prizewinners.* T **318** *and similar horiz designs. Multicoloured. Chalk-surfaced paper.* P 15×15.

928	28p. Type **318**		60	75
	a. Pair. Nos. 928/9		1·10	1·50
	b. Booklet pane. Nos. 928/9 and 930×2 with margins all round		3·00	
	c. Booklet pane. Nos. 928/31 with margins all round		3·00	
	d. Booklet pane. Nos. 928/30 with margins all round		3·00	
929	28p. Samuel Beckett (author) and pair of boots		60	75
930	32p. Sean MacBride (human rights campaigner) and peace doves		70	75
	a. Booklet pane. Nos. 930 and 931×2 with margins all round		3·00	
931	52p. William Butler Yeats (poet) and poem		1·10	1·75
928/31		*Set of 4*	2·75	3·50

Nos. 928/9 were printed together, *se-tenant*, in horizontal and vertical pairs throughout the sheet.

The booklet panes also exist overprinted for Regional Stamp Shows at Waterford, Galway, Athlone and Kilkenny.

(Des Pamela Leonard (No. 932), Q Design (others). Litho Irish Security Stamp Ptg Ltd)

1994 (17 Nov). *Christmas.* T **319** *and similar vert designs. Chalk-surfaced paper.* P 14×15.

932	28p. Nativity		70	60
	a. Sheetlet. No. 932×13		8·00	
933	28p. Type **319**		70	60
934	32p. Flight into Egypt (wood carving)		80	70
935	52p. Nativity (ivory plaque)		1·10	2·00
932/5		*Set of 4*	3·00	3·50

No. 932 was only issued in sheetlets of 13 stamps and two labels (at the centre of rows 1 and 2) sold at £3.36 providing a discount of 28p. off the face value of the stamps.

320 Tree of Hearts

321 West Clare Railway Steam Locomotive No. 1 *Kilkee* at Kilrush Station

(Des Bridget Flinn. Litho Irish Security Stamp Ptg Ltd)

1995 (24 Jan). *Greetings Stamps.* T **320** *and similar vert designs. Multicoloured. Chalk-surfaced paper.* P 14×15.

936	32p. Type **320**		80	95
	a. Booklet pane. Nos. 936/7		3·00	
937	32p. Teddy bear holding balloon		80	95

938	32p. Clown juggling hearts			80	95
939	32p. Bouquet of flowers			80	95
936/9			Set of 4	3·00	3·50

Nos. 937/9 were only available from £2.56 stamp booklets containing two examples of No. 936a. This pane, which also includes 8 small greetings labels, exists in two different forms with either No. 936 at left and No. 938 at right or No. 937 at left and No. 939 at right. In each instance the right-hand stamp is imperforate at right.

(Des Bridget Flynn. Litho Irish Security Stamp Ptg Ltd)

1995 (24 Jan). *Chinese New Year ("Year of the Pig"). P* 14×15.
MS940	137×74 mm. Nos. 936, 938/9			2·25	2·75

The example of No. 939 in the above miniature sheet is imperforate at right.

(Des C. Rycraft. Litho Irish Security Stamp Ptg Ltd)

1995 (28 Feb). *Transport. Narrow Gauge Railways. T* **321** *and similar horiz designs. Multicoloured. Chalk-surfaced paper. P* 15×14.
941	28p. Type **321**			75	60
942	32p. County Donegal Railway tank locomotive No. 2 *Blanche* at Donegal Station			90	90
943	38p. Cork and Muskerry Railway tank locomotive No. 1 *City of Cork* on Western Road, Cork			1·25	1·75
944	52p. Cavan and Leitrim tank locomotive No. 3 *Lady Edith* on Arigna Tramway			1·75	2·50
941/4			Set of 4	4·25	5·25
MS945	127×83 mm. Nos. 941/4			4·25	5·25

No. **MS945** also exists with the "Singapore '95" International Stamp Exhibition logo added.

322 English and Irish Rugby Players

(Des C. Harrison. Litho Walsall)

1995 (6 Apr). *World Cup Rugby Championship, South Africa. T* **322** *and similar horiz design. Multicoloured. Chalk-surfaced paper. P* 14.
946	32p. Type **322**			75	75
947	52p. Australian and Irish players			1·25	1·75
MS948	108×77 mm. £1 Type **322**			2·50	2·75

No. **MS948** also exists overprinted for Regional Stamp Shows at Limerick and Letterkenny.

323 Peace Dove and Skyscrapers

324 Soldiers of the Irish Brigade and Memorial Cross

(Des R. Ballagh)

1995 (6 Apr). *Europa. Peace and Freedom. T* **323** *and similar horiz design. Multicoloured. Chalk-surfaced paper.* (a) *Litho Irish Security Stamp Ptg Ltd. P* 15×14.
949	32p. Type **323**			85	75
950	44p. Peace dove and map of Europe and North Africa			1·40	2·00

(b) *Litho Printset Cambec Pty Ltd, Melbourne. Self-adhesive. P* 11½.
951	32p. Type **323**			90	90
952	32p. As No. 950			90	90

Nos. 949/50 were issued in sheetlets of 10 (2×5) with illustrated left margins.

Nos. 951/2 are smaller, 34½×23 mm, and occur, *se-tenant*, in pairs or rolls of 100 with the surplus self-adhesive paper around each stamps removed.

(Des E. Daniels. Photo Belgian Post Office Ptg Wks, Malines)

1995 (15 May). *250th Anniv of Battle of Fontenoy. Chalk-surfaced paper. P* 11½.
953	**324**	32p. multicoloured			80	80

325 Irish Brigade, French Army, 1745   **326** Guglielmo Marconi and Original Radio Transmitter

(Des D. McAllister. Litho Irish Security Stamp Ptg Ltd)

1995 (15 May). *Military Uniforms. T* **325** *and similar vert designs. Multicoloured. Chalk-surfaced paper. P* 14×15.
954	28p. Type **325**			70	60
	a. Booklet pane. Nos. 954/5, each × 2		3·00	
	b. Booklet pane. Nos. 954/5 and 957/8		3·00	
	c. Booklet pane. Nos. 954/5 and 957		3·00	
	d. Booklet pane. Nos. 954/5 and 958		3·00	
955	32p. Tercio Irlanda, Spanish army in Flanders, 1605			80	75
956	32p. Royal Dublin Fusiliers, 1914			80	75
957	38p. St. Patrick's Battalion, Papal Army, 1860			1·10	1·25
958	52p. 69th Regiment, New York State Militia, 1861			1·60	1·75
954/8			Set of 5	4·50	4·50

Booklet panes Nos. 954a/b come with the two right-hand stamps (Nos. 954/5 or 955 and 958) imperforate at right.

The booklet panes also exist overprinted for Regional Stamp Shows at Sligo, Waterford and Galway and for "Stampa '95" (two panes).

(Des E. Jünger (No. 959), S. Young (No. 960). Litho Irish Security Stamp Ptg Ltd)

1995 (8 June). *Centenary of Radio. T* **326** *and similar horiz design. Multicoloured. Chalk-surfaced paper. P* 13½.
959	32p. Type **326**			80	1·00
	a. Pair. Nos. 959/60			1·60	2·00
960	32p. Traditional radio dial			80	1·00

Nos. 959/60 were printed together, *se-tenant*, in horizontal and vertical pairs throughout the sheet.

327 Bartholomew Mosse (founder) and Hospital Building

(Des A. May (No. 961), S. Woulfe Flanagan (No. 962), Q Design (No. 963), Creative Inputs (No. 964). Litho Questa (Nos. 961/2) or Irish Security Stamp Ptg Ltd (others))

1995 (27 July). *Anniversaries. T* **327** *and similar multicoloured designs. Chalk-surfaced paper. P* 15×14 (*Nos.* 961), 14½ (*No.* 962), 14½×14 (*No.* 963) *or* 13½ (*No.* 964).

961	28p. Type **327** (250th anniv of Rotunda Hospital)		70	70
962	32p. St. Patrick's House, Maynooth College (Bicent) (25×41 *mm*)		80	80
963	32p. Laurel wreath and map of Europe (50th anniv of end of Second World War)		80	80
964	52p. Geological map of Ireland (150th anniv of Geological Survey of Ireland) (32½×32½ *mm*)		1·25	1·50
961/4		*Set of* 4	3·25	3·50

328 Natterjack Toad   **329** *Crinum moorei*

(Des I. Loe. Litho Irish Security Stamp Ptg Ltd)

1995 (1 Sept). *Reptiles and Amphibians. T* **328** *and similar horiz designs. Chalk-surfaced paper.* (a) *P* 15×14.

965	32p. Type **328**		1·00	1·25
	a. Horiz strip. Nos. 965/8		3·50	
966	32p. Common Lizards		1·00	1·25
967	32p. Smooth Newts		1·00	1·25
968	32p. Common Frog		1·00	1·25
965/8		*Set of* 4	3·50	4·50

(b) *Self-adhesive. P* 9½.

969	32p. Type **328**		1·00	1·25
970	32p. Common Lizard		1·00	1·25
971	32p. Smooth Newt		1·00	1·25
972	32p. Common Frog		1·00	1·25
969/72		*Set of* 4	3·50	4·50

Nos. 965/8 were printed together, *se-tenant*, in horizontal strips of 4 with the backgrounds forming a composite design. Nos. 969/72 are smaller, 34×23 mm, and occur, *se-tenant*, in strips of 4 or rolls of 100 with the surplus self-adhesive paper around each stamp removed.

(Des Frances Poskitt. Litho Irish Security Stamp Ptg Ltd)

1995 (9 Oct). *Bicentenary of National Botanic Gardens, Glasnevin. Flowers. T* **329** *and similar vert designs. Multicoloured. Chalk-surfaced paper. P* 14×15.

973	32p. Type **329**		85	70
	a. Booklet pane. Nos. 973×2 and 974/5		4·50	
	b. Booklet pane. Nos. 973/5		4·50	
974	38p. *Sarracenia × moorei*		1·10	1·10
975	44p. *Solanum crispum* "Glasnevin"		1·50	2·25
973/5		*Set of* 3	3·00	3·50

Booklet panes Nos. 973a/b come from £2.60 stamp booklets and have the outer edges of the pane imperforate so that examples of each value exist imperforate on one or two sides.

330 Anniversary Logo and Irish United Nations Soldier

(Des Jarlath Hayes. Litho Enschedé)

1995 (19 Oct). *50th Anniv of United Nations. T* **330** *and similar horiz design. Multicoloured. Chalk-surfaced paper. P* 13×13½.

976	32p. Type **330**		80	70
977	52p. Emblem and "UN"		1·25	1·40

Nos. 976/7 were each issued in sheets of 10 (2×5) with enlarged illustrated left margins.

331 "Adoration of the Shepherds" (illuminated manuscript) (Benedetto Bardone)

332 Zig and Zag on Heart

(Des Q Design. Litho Irish Security Stamp Ptg Ltd)

1995 (16 Nov). *Christmas. T* **331** *and similar horiz designs. Multicoloured. Chalk-surfaced paper. P* 15×14.

978	28p. Adoration of the Magi		70	65
	a. Sheetlet. No. 978×13		8·25	
979	28p. Type **331**		70	65
980	32p. "Adoration of the Magi" (illuminated manuscript) (Bardone)		80	70
981	52p. "The Holy Family" (illuminated manuscript) (Bardone)		1·40	1·60
978/81		*Set of* 4	3·25	3·25

No. 978 was only issued in sheetlets of 13 stamps and two labels (at centre of rows 1 and 2) sold at £3.36 providing a discount of 28p. off the face value of the stamps.

(Des Double Z Enterprises. Litho Irish Security Stamp Ptg Ltd)

1996 (23 Jan). *Greetings Stamps. T* **332** *and similar vert designs. Multicoloured. Chalk-surfaced paper. P* 14×15.

982	32p. Type **332**		95	95
	a. Booklet pane. Nos. 982/5		3·50	
983	32p. Zig and Zag waving		95	95
984	32p. Zig and Zag in space suits		95	95
985	32p. Zig and Zag wearing hats		95	95
982/5		*Set of* 4	3·50	3·50

Nos. 983/5 were only issued in £2.56 stamp booklets. No. 982 was available from sheets and booklets.

Booklet pane No. 982a, which also includes eight small greetings labels, exists in two different forms with either No. 982 or 984 at right. In each instance the right-hand stamp is imperforate at right.

(Des Double Z Enterprises. Litho Irish Security Stamp Ptg Ltd)

1996 (23 Jan). *Chinese New Year* ("Year of the Rat"). *Chalk-surfaced paper. P* 14×15.

MS986	130×74 mm. Nos. 982, 984/5		3·00	3·00

The example of No. 982 in No. **MS**986 is imperforate at right. No. **MS**986 also exists overprinted for the Collectors' Road Show at Kilkenny.

333 Wheelchair Athlete   **334** Before the Start, Fairyhouse Race Course

(Des C. Harrison. Litho Irish Security Stamp Ptg Ltd)

1996 (1 Feb). *Olympic and Paralympic Games, Atlanta. T* **333** *and similar vert. designs. Multicoloured. Chalk-surfaced paper. P* 14×15.

987	28p. Type **333**				70	65
988	32p. Running	..	..	..	80	80
	a. Strip of 3. Nos. 988/90		..	2·25		
989	32p. Throwing the discus	..			80	80
990	32p. Single kayak ..		..	..	80	80
987/90		..	..	*Set of* 4	2·75	2·75

Nos. 988/90 were printed together, *se-tenant*, as horizontal and vertical strips of 3 in sheets of 9.

(Des P. Curling and Q Design. Litho Irish Security Stamp Ptg Ltd)

1996 (12 Mar). *Irish Horse Racing. T* **334** *and similar horiz designs. Multicoloured. Chalk-surfaced paper. P* 15×14.

991	28p. Type **334**	..	..		70	65
	a. Booklet pane. Nos. 991×2 and 992/3		4·25			
992	32p. Steeplechase, Punchestown	..		80	80
	a. Pair. Nos. 992/3	..	..	1·60	1·60	
	b. Booklet pane. Nos. 992/5	..	4·25			
	c. Booklet pane. Nos. 992×2 and 994	4·25			
993	32p. On the Flat, The Curragh	..	80	80	
	a. Booklet pane. Nos. 993×2 and 995	4·25			
994	38p. Steeplechase, Galway	..	..	1·25	1·25
995	52p. After the race, Leopardstown	..	1·50	1·50
991/5		..	..	*Set of* 4	4·50	4·50

Nos. 992/3 were printed together, *se-tenant*, in horizontal and vertical pairs throughout the sheet.

Booklet pane Nos. 991a, 992b/c and 993a come from £4.92 stamp booklets with the right-hand edge of the panes imperforate. The complete booklet contains two examples of No. 992 and each of Nos. 991, 993 and 995 imperforate at right.

The booklet panes also exist overprinted for Collectors' Road Shows at Cork (No. 992c), Limerick (No. 991a) or Sligo (No. 993a) and for "Stampa '96" (No. 992c).

For designs as Nos. 992/3 in miniature sheet see No. **MS**1003.

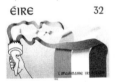

335 Irish and French Coloured Ribbons merging

336 Louie Bennett (suffragette)

(Des R. Ballagh. Litho Irish Security Stamp Ptg Ltd)

1996 (12 Mar). *"L'Imaginaire Irlandais" Festival of Contemporary Irish Arts, France. Chalk-surfaced paper. P* 15×14.

996	**335**	32p. multicoloured	..	..	80	80

(Des S. Young)

1996 (2 Apr). *Europa. Famous Women. T* **336** *and similar horiz design. Chalk-surfaced paper.*

     (*a*) *Litho Questa. P* 15×14

997	**336**	32p. deep reddish violet	..		80	70
998	–	44p. myrtle-green	..	..	1·10	1·25

     (*b*) *Litho Irish Security Stamp Ptg Ltd. Self-adhesive. P* 9½

999	**336**	32p. deep reddish violet	..	80	1·00
1000	–	32p. dull green	..	..	80	1·00

Design:—Nos. 998, 1000, Lady Augusta Gregory (playwright).

Nos. 997/8 were each issued in sheetlets of 10 (2×5) with enlarged illustrated left margins.

Nos. 999/1000 are smaller, 34×23 mm, and occur, *se-tenant*, in rolls of 100 with the surplus self-adhesive paper around each stamp removed.

337 Newgrange Passage Tomb (Boyne Valley World Heritage Site)

(Des L. Belton (28p.), Q Design (32p.). Litho Walsall)

1996 (2 Apr). *Anniversaries and Events. T* **337** *and similar horiz design. Chalk-surfaced paper. P* 14.

1001	28p. grey-brown and black	..	..	85	60
1002	32p. multicoloured	..	..	..	90	90

Designs:—32p. Children playing (50th anniv of U.N.I.C.E.F.).

(Litho Irish Security Stamp Printing Ltd)

1996 (18 May). *"CHINA '96" 9th Asian International Stamp Exhibition, Peking. Sheet* 120×95 *mm containing Nos.* 992/3. *Chalk-surfaced paper. P* 15×14.

MS1003	32p. Steeplechase, Punchestown; 32p. On the Flat, The Curragh	..	..	2·25	2·75

ÉIRE 32

TOURIST TROPHY · IRISH WINNERS

338 Stanley Woods

Michael Davitt 1846-1906

339 Michael Davitt (founder of The Land League)

(Des J. Dunne. Litho Questa)

1996 (30 May). *Isle of Man Tourist Trophy Motorcycle Races. Irish Winners. T* **338** *and similar horiz designs. Multicoloured. Chalk-surfaced paper. P* 14.

1004	32p. Type **339**	..	..	80	70
1005	44p. Artie Bell	..	..	1·25	1·40
1006	50p. Alec Bennett	..	..	1·50	1·60
1007	52p. Joey and Robert Dunlop	..	1·50	1·60
1004/7		..	..	*Set of* 4	4·50	4·75
MS1008	100×70 mm. 50p. As 52p.	..	1·25	1·50

No. **MS**1008 also exists overprinted for "Stampa '96" and for the Collectors' Road Show at Dundalk.

(Des R. Ballagh (28p.), J. Tobin (32p.), C. Harrison (38p.), L. Belton (52p.). Litho Enschedé)

1996 (4 July). *Anniversaries and Events. T* **339** *and similar multicoloured designs. Chalk-surfaced paper. P* 13½×13 (28p.) *or* 13×13½ (*others*).

1009	28p. Type **339** (150th birth anniv)	..	70	60
1010	32p. Presidency logo (Ireland's Presidency of European Union) (*horiz*) ..		80	70
1011	38p. Thomas McLaughlin (hydro-electric engineer) and Ardnacrusha Power Station (Birth centenary) (*horiz*)	..	1·00	1·10
1012	52p. Mechanical peat harvester (50th anniv of Bord na Móna) (*horiz*)	..	1·60	1·75
1009/12		..	..	..	*Set of* 4	3·75	3·75

MINIMUM PRICE

The minimum price quote is 10p which represents a handling charge rather than a basis for valuing common stamps. For further notes about prices see introductory pages.

340 Coastal Patrol Vessel   **341** Blind Woman
with Child

(Des G. Fallon. Litho Irish Security Stamp Ptg Ltd)

1996 (18 July). *50th Anniv of Irish Naval Service. T* **340** *and similar multicoloured designs. Chalk-surfaced paper. P* 14×15 (52p.) *or* 15×14 (*others*).
1013 32p. Type **340** 80 70
    a. Booklet pane. No. 1013×3 .. .. 2·75
    b. Booklet pane. Nos. 1013/15 .. 2·75
1014 44p. Corvette .. .. .. 1·40 1·50
1015 52p. Motor torpedo boat (*vert*) .. 1·50 1·60
1013/15 .. .. .. *Set of 3* 3·25 3·50
Booklet panes Nos. 1013a/b come from £2.24 stamp booklets. Stamps from No. 1013a have either one or two adjacent sides imperforate and those from No. 1013b are imperforate at foot (32, 44p.) or at right and foot (52p.).
    The booklet panes also exist overprinted for "Stampa '96" (No. 1013b) or for the Collectors' Road Shows at Galway (No. 1013b) and Waterford (No. 1013a).

(Des E. Patton. Litho Irish Security Stamp Ptg Ltd)

1996 (3 Sept). *People with Disabilities. T* **341** *and similar vert design. Multicoloured. Chalk-surfaced paper. P* 14×15.
1016 28p. Type **341** 55 60
    a. Pair. Nos. 1016/7 .. .. 1·10
1017 28p. Man in wheelchair playing bowls .. 55 60
Nos. 1016/17 were printed together, *se-tenant*, in horizontal and vertical pairs throughout the sheet.

342 Green-winged Teal

(Des R. Ward. Litho Irish Security Stamp Ptg Ltd)

1996 (24 Sept). *Freshwater Ducks. T* **342** *and similar horiz designs. Multicoloured. Chalk-surfaced paper. P* 15×14.
1018 32p. Type **342** 85 70
1019 38p. Common Shoveler .. .. 1·00 1·00
1020 44p. European Wigeon .. .. 1·25 1·25
1021 52p. Mallard .. .. .. 1·50 1·50
1018/21 .. .. .. *Set of 4* 4·25 4·00
MS1022 127×85 mm. Nos. 1018/21 .. 4·25 4·50

343 Scene from *Man of Aran*   **344** Visit of the
Magi

(Des J. Reddy. Litho Irish Security Stamp Ptg Ltd)

1996 (17 Oct). *Centenary of Irish Cinema. T* **343** *and similar horiz designs. Multicoloured. Chalk-surfaced paper. P* 13½.
1023 32p. Type **343** 85 90
    a. Strip of 4. Nos. 1023/6 .. .. 3·00
1024 32p. *My Left Foot* 85 90
1025 32p. *The Commitments* 85 90
1026 32p. *The Field* 85 90
1023/6 .. .. .. *Set of 4* 3·00 3·25
Nos. 1023/6 were printed together, *se-tenant*, in vertical and horizontal strips of 4 throughout the sheet.

(Des T. Monaghan (No. 1027), E. Patton (others). Litho Irish Security Stamp Ptg Ltd)

1996 (19 Nov). *Christmas. T* **344** *and similar vert designs from 16th-century Book of Hours (Nos.* 1028/30). *Multicoloured. Chalk-surfaced paper (Nos.* 1028/30). *P* 14×15.
1027 28p. The Holy Family 75 60
    a. Sheetlet. No. 1027×15 .. .. 10·00
1028 28p. Type **344** 60 60
1029 32p. The Annunciation 80 75
1030 52p. The Shepherds receiving news of Christ's birth .. .. 1·40 1·60
1027/30 .. .. .. *Set of 4* 3·25 3·25
No. 1027 was only issued in sheetlets of 15 stamps sold at £3.92 providing a discount of 28p. off the face value of the stamps.

345 Magpie   **346** Pair of Doves

(Des K. Mullarney)

1997 (16 Jan)–**99**. *Birds. T* **345** *and similar multicoloured designs.*

(a) Litho Walsall (*Nos.* 1038ac, 1053ac, 1054ac, 1055ac, 1057ac, 1058ac) *or Irish Security Stamp Ptg Ltd* (*others*). *Chalk-surfaced paper* (1p., 2p., 4p., 10p., 20p., 30p. (*Nos.* 1039/52), £5) *or ordinary paper* (*others*). *P* 15×14 (5p., 28p., 40p., 50p., £1, £5) *or* 14×15 (*others*)

(i) *Size* 21×24 *mm* (*vert*) *or* 24×21 *mm* (*horiz*)
1031 1p. Type **345** (27.8.97) 10 10
1032 2p. Gannet (27.8.97) 10 10
1033 4p. Corncrake (27.8.97) 10 10
    a. Ordinary paper (3.98) 20 10
1034 5p. Wood Pigeon (*horiz*) (2.4.98) .. 10 10
    a. Chalk-surfaced paper (9.98) .. 20 10
1035 10p. Kingfisher (27.8.97) 20 25
1036 20p. Lapwing (27.8.97) 35 40
1037 28p. Blue Tit (*horiz*) 50 55
    a. Chalk-surfaced paper (10.97) .. 50 55
1038 30p. Blackbird (2.4.98) 55 60
    a. Chalk-surfaced paper (9.98) .. 80 60
    ab. Booklet pane. Nos. 1038a and 1039, each × 5 (4.9.98) .. .. 5·50
    ac. Perf 14 (phosphor frame) (17.11.98) 55 60
    ap. Phosphor frame (16.2.99) .. 55 60
    aq. Sheetlet. Nos. 1038ap, 1039p and 1040/52 (16.2.99) .. 8·00
    ar. Booklet pane. Nos. 1038ap and 1039p, each × 5 (3.99) .. .. 5·50
1039 30p. Goldcrest (4.9.98) 55 60
    p. Phosphor frame (16.2.99) .. 55 60
1040 30p. Stonechat (*phosphor frame*) (16.2.99) 55 60
1041 30p. Lapwing (*phosphor frame*) (16.2.99) 55 60
1042 30p. Gannet (*phosphor frame*) (16.2.99) .. 55 60
1043 30p. Corncrake (*phosphor frame*) (16.2.99) 55 60
1044 30p. Type **345** (*phosphor frame*) (16.2.99) 55 60
1045 30p. Kingfisher (*phosphor frame*) (16.2.99) 55 60

1046	30p. Peregrine Falcon (*phosphor frame*) (16.2.99)		55	60
1047	30p. Barn Owl (*phosphor frame*) (16.2.99)		55	60
1048	30p. Robin (*phosphor frame*) (16.2.99)		55	60
1049	30p. Song Thrush (*phosphor frame*) (16.2.99)		55	60
1050	30p. Wren (*phosphor frame*) (16.2.99)		55	60
1051	30p. Pied Wagtail (*phosphor frame*) (16.2.99)		55	60
1052	30p. Puffin (*phosphor frame*) (16.2.99)		55	60
1053	32p. Robin		60	65
	a. Chalk-surfaced paper (10.97)		60	65
	ac. Perf 14 (*phosphor frame*) (17.11.98)		60	65
	ad. Phosphor frame (30.6.99)		60	65
	ae. Booklet pane. No. 1053ad×5, plus 5 airmail labels		3·00	
1054	35p. Stonechat (2.4.98)		65	70
	a. Chalk-surfaced paper (4.98)		1·10	70
	ac. Perf 14 (*phosphor frame*) (17.11.98)		65	70
1055	40p. Ringed Plover (*horiz*) (2.4.98)		70	75
	ac. Perf 14. Chalk-surfaced paper (*phosphor frame*) (17.11.98)		70	75
1056	44p. Puffin		80	85
1057	45p. Song Thrush (2.4.98)		80	85
	a. Chalk-surfaced paper (9.98)		1·40	85
	ac. Perf 14 (*phosphor frame*) (17.11.98)		80	85
	ad. Phosphor frame (18.5.99)		80	85
	ae. Booklet pane. No. 1057ad×4, plus 4 labels (30.6.99)		3·25	
1058	50p. European Sparrow Hawk (*horiz*) (2.4.98)		90	95
	a. Chalk-surfaced paper (8.98)		1·50	95
	ac. Perf 14 (phosphor frame) (17.11.98)		90	95
1059	52p. Barn Owl		95	1·00

(ii) Size 24×45 mm (vert) or 45×24 mm (horiz)

1060	£1 Greenland White-fronted Goose		1·75	1·90
	a. Chalk-surfaced paper (11.98)		2·50	1·90
1061	£2 Pintail (*horiz*) (2.4.98)		3·50	3·75
1062	£5 Shelduck (27.8.97)		9·00	9·25
	a. Ordinary paper (9.98)		13·00	9·25
1031/62		*Set of 32*	28·00	30·00

(b) Booklet stamps. Litho Irish Security Stamp Ptg Ltd. Size 21×17 (5p.) or 17×21 mm (others). Chalk-surfaced paper (4p., 30p. (No. 1083), 32p.) or ordinary paper (others). P 14×15 (5p.) or 15×14 (others)

1080	4p. Corncrake (6.12.97)		10	10
	a. Booklet pane. Nos. 1080 and 1085×3		1·75	
1081	5p. Wood Pigeon (*horiz*) (2.4.98)		10	10
	a. Booklet pane. Nos. 1081×2 and 1082×3 plus label		1·75	
	b. Chalk-surfaced paper (16.2.99)		10	10
	ba. Booklet pane. Nos. 1081b×2 and 1083×3 plus label		1·75	
1082	30p. Blackbird (2.4.98)		55	60
1083	30p. Goldcrest ("all-over" phosphor) (16.2.99)		55	60
1084	32p. Robin (6.3.97)		60	65
1085	32p. Peregrine Falcon (6.12.97)		60	65

(c) Self-adhesive. Size 25×30 mm.

(i) Litho Irish Stamp Security Ptg Ltd. P 9×10

1086	30p. Goldcrest (2.4.98)		75	65
	a. Vert pair. Nos. 1086/7		1·50	1·25
	p. Phosphor frame (14.12.98)		55	65
	pa. Vert pair. Nos. 1086p/7p		1·10	1·25
1087	30p. Blackbird (2.4.98)		75	65
	p. Phosphor frame (14.12.98)		55	65
1088	32p. Peregrine Falcon (6.3.97)		75	65
	a. Vert pair. Nos. 1088/9		1·50	1·25
1089	32p. Robin (6.3.97)		75	65

(ii) Litho SNP Cambec, Melbourne. P 11½

1090	30p. Goldcrest (2.4.98)		75	65
	a. Vert pair. Nos. 1090/1		1·50	1·25
	p. Phosphor frame (17.11.98)		55	65
	pa. Vert pair. Nos. 1090p/1p		1·10	1·25
1091	30p. Blackbird (2.4.98)		75	65
	p. Phosphor frame (17.11.98)		55	65
1092	32p. Peregrine Falcon (4.97)		75	1·25
	a. Vert pair. Nos. 1092/3		1·50	2·50
1093	32p. Robin (4.97)		75	1·25

No. 1039 was only issued in £3 stamp booklets which show the upper and lower edges of the pane imperforate and a margin at either end.

The sheet stamps with phosphor frames and No. 1038ar show the actual designs slightly reduced to provide a clear 2 mm border on which the phosphor frame appears.

The sheetlet, No. 1038aq, repeats the vertical designs from other values in the set. The designs showing the Wren and Pied Wagtail only occur in the sheetlet. It also exists overprinted for the Collectors' Road Show at Limerick.

Nos. 748bb (containing No. 1084), 1080a, 1081a and 1081ab show the upper and lower edges of the panes imperforate. Booklet panes Nos. 1053ae and 1057ae show the stamps as a horizontal row with margins on three sides and the airmail labels attached at right. On booklet pane No. 1081ba the three 30p. have "all-over" phosphor, but this does not extend to the two 5p. stamps or the label.

Nos. 1086/7, 1088/9, 1090/1 and 1092/3 were produced in rolls of 100, each containing two designs. Those printed by Irish Stamp Security Ptg Ltd retain the surplus self-adhesive paper around each stamp, but this was removed for those produced in Australia.

Nos. 1086p/7p show the actual designs slightly reduced and the inscriptions repositioned to provide a clear 2 mm border on which the phosphor frame appears.

For £2 value in miniature sheet see No. **MS**1131.

(Des Double Z Enterprises. Litho Irish Security Stamp Ptg Ltd)

1997 (28 Jan). *Greetings Stamps. T 346 and similar vert designs. Multicoloured. Chalk-surfaced paper. P 14×15.*

1100	32p. Type **346**		85	90
	a. Booklet pane. Nos. 1100/3		3·00	
1101	32p. Cow jumping over moon		85	90
1102	32p. Pig going to market		85	90
1103	32p. Cockerel		85	90
1100/3		*Set of 4*	3·00	3·25

Nos. 1101/3 were only issued in £2.56 stamp booklets. No. 1100 was available from sheets and booklets.

Booklet pane No. 1100a, which also includes eight small greetings labels, exists in two forms with No. 1101 either at left or right. In each instance the right-hand stamp, No. 1101 or No. 1103, is imperforate at right.

(Des Double Z Enterprises. Litho Irish Security Stamp Ptg Ltd)

1997 (28 Jan). *"HONG KONG '97" International Stamp Exhibition. Chinese New Year ("Year of the Ox"). Chalk-surfaced paper. P 14×15.*

MS1104	124×74 mm. Nos. 1101/3		2·40	2·40

The example of No. 1103 in No. **MS**1104 is imperforate at right.

No. **MS**1104 also exists overprinted for the Collectors' Road Show at Limerick.

347 Troops on Parade   **348** Grey Seals

(Des Q Design. Litho Irish Security Stamp Ptg Ltd)

1997 (18 Feb–6 Dec). *75th Anniv of Irish Free State. T 347 and similar horiz designs. Multicoloured. Chalk-surfaced paper. P 15×14.*

1105	28p. Page from the "Annals of the Four Masters", quill and 1944 ½d. O'Clery stamp (27 Aug)		55	55
1106	32p. Type **347**		60	65
	a. Pair. Nos. 1106/7		1·25	1·25
1107	32p. The Dail, national flag and Constitution		60	65
1108	32p. Athlete, footballer and hurling players (3 Apr)		60	65
	a. Pair. Nos. 1108/9		1·25	1·25

1109	32p.	Singer, violinist and bodhran player (3 Apr)	60	65
1110	32p.	Stained glass window and 1929 9d. O'Connell stamp (27 Aug)	60	60
1111	32p.	G.P.O., Dublin, and 1923 2d. map stamp (6 Dec)	60	60
1112	52p.	Police personnel and Garda badge	1·00	1·25
	a.	Pair. Nos. 1112/13	2·00	2·50
1113	52p.	The Four Courts and Scales of Justice	1·00	1·25
1114	52p.	Currency, blueprint and food-processing plant (3 Apr)	1·00	1·25
	a.	Pair. Nos. 1114/15	2·00	2·50
1115	52p.	Books, palette and Seamus Heaney manuscript (3 Apr)	1·00	1·25
1116	52p.	Air Lingus airliner and 1965 1s. 5d air stamp (27 Aug)	1·00	95
1105/16		*Set of* 12	8·25	9·00
MS1117		174×209 mm. As Nos. 1105/16, but each with face value of 32p. (6 Dec)	6·50	7·50

Nos. 1106/7, 1108/9, 1112/13 and 1114/15 were each printed together, *se-tenant*, in horiz or vert pairs throughout the sheets.

(Des Rosemary Davis. Litho Irish Security Stamp Ptg Ltd)

1997 (6 Mar). *Marine Mammals. T* **348** *and similar multicoloured designs. Chalk-surfaced paper. P* 14×15 (28p., 32p.) *or* 15×14 (*others*).

1118	28p.	Type **348**	75	60
1119	32p.	Bottle-nosed Dolphins	85	80
1120	44p.	Harbour Porpoises (*horiz*)	1·25	1·40
1121	52p.	Killer Whale (*horiz*)	1·40	1·50
1118/21		*Set of* 4	3·75	3·75
MS1122		150×68 mm. As Nos. 1118/21. P 15	3·75	3·75

No. **MS**1122 also exists overprinted for the Collectors' Road Show at Dublin.

349 Dublin Silver Penny of 997

(Des Creative Inputs. Litho Irish Security Stamp Ptg Ltd)

1997 (3 Apr). *Millenary of Irish Coinage. Chalk-surfaced paper. P* 15×14.

1123	**349**	32p. multicoloured	65	65

350 "The Children of Lir"

(Des P. Lynch)

1997 (14 May). *Europa. Tales and Legends. T* **350** *and similar horiz design. Multicoloured.* (a) *Litho Walsall. Chalk-surfaced paper. P* 14.

1124	32p.	Type **350**	70	60
1125	44p.	Oisin and Niamh	1·00	1·10

(*b*) *Litho Irish Security Stamp Ptg Ltd. Self-adhesive. P* 9½.

1126	32p.	Type **350**	70	70
	a.	Horiz pair. Nos. 1126/7	1·40	1·40
1127	32p.	Oisin and Niamh	70	70
1124/7		*Set of* 4	2·75	2·75

Nos. 1124/5 were each issued in sheetlets of 10 (2×5) with enlarged illustrated left margins.

Nos. 1126/7, which are smaller 36×25 mm, occur in rolls of 100.

AN GORTA MÓR

351 Emigrants waiting to board Ship

(Des Q Design. Litho Irish Security Stamp Ptg Ltd)

1997 (14 May). *150th Anniv of The Great Famine. T* **351** *and similar horiz designs. Chalk-surfaced paper. P* 15×14.

1128	28p.	dp dull blue, verm & pale yellow-ochre	75	60
1129	32p.	reddish orange, deep dull blue and pale yellow-ochre	90	70
1130	52p.	brown, dp dull blue & pale yell-ochre	1·40	1·40
1128/30		*Set of* 3	2·75	2·40

Designs—32p. Family and dying child; 52p. Irish Society of Friends soup kitchen.

(Des K. Mullarney. Litho Irish Security Stamp Ptg Ltd)

1997 (29 May). *"Pacific '97" International Stamp Exhibition, San Francisco. Sheet,* 100×70 *mm, containing No.* 1061. *Multicoloured. Chalk-surfaced paper. P* 14.

MS1131	£2	Pintail (48×26 *mm*)	4·50	5·00

352 Kate O'Brien (novelist) (birth centenary)

353 The Baily Lighthouse

(Des Creative Inputs. Litho Irish Security Stamp Ptg Ltd (No. 1133) or Walsall (others))

1997 (1 July). *Anniversaries. T* **352** *and similar vert designs. Multicoloured. Chalk-surfaced paper. P* 14×15 (*No.* 1133), 14½ (*No.* 1134) *or* 14 (*others*).

1132	28p.	Type **352**	60	60
1133	28p.	St. Columba crossing to Iona (stained glass window) (1400th death anniv)	60	60
1134	32p.	"Daniel O'Connell" (J. Haverty) (politician) (150th death anniv) (27×49 *mm*)	70	70
1135	52p.	"John Wesley" (N. Hone) (founder of Methodism) (250th anniv of first visit to Ireland)	1·25	1·40
1132/5		*Set of* 4	2·75	3·00

(Des Design Image. Litho Irish Security Stamp Ptg Ltd)

1997 (1 July). *Lighthouses. T* **353** *and similar multicoloured designs. Chalk-surfaced paper. P* 15×14 (32p.) *or* 14×15 (*others*).

1136	32p.	Type **353**	70	80
	a.	Pair. Nos. 1136/7	1·40	1·60
	b.	Booklet pane. Nos. 1136×2 and 1137	1·60	
	c.	Booklet pane. Nos. 1136/7, each × 2	2·00	
	d.	Perf 15	1·10	1·40
	e.	Booklet pane. Nos. 1136d/9d	4·00	
1137	32p.	Tarbert	70	80
	d.	Perf 15	1·10	1·40
1138	38p.	Hookhead (*vert*)	75	85
	d.	Perf 15	1·10	1·40
	da.	Booklet pane. Nos. 1138d/9d	2·00	

1139	50p. The Fastnet (vert)	.. .. ..	1·10	1·25
	d. Perf 15	.. .. ..	1·10	1·40
1136/9	.. .. ..	Set of 4	3·00	3·25

Nos. 1136/7 were printed together, se-tenant, in horizontal or vertical pairs throughout the sheet.

Nos. 1136d/9d only exist from booklet panes Nos. 1136da and 1138da.

The booklet panes also exist overprinted for Collectors' Road Shows at Sligo (No. 1136b), Tralee (No. 1138da), Galway (No. 1136c) or Limerick (No. 1136da) and also for "Stampa '97" (Nos. 1136b/c, 1136da and 1138da).

354 Commemorative Cross

355 Dracula and Bat

(Des L. Rafael. Litho Irish Security Stamp Ptg Ltd)

1997 (12 Sept). *Ireland–Mexico Joint Issue. 150th Anniv of Mexican St. Patrick's Battalion. Ordinary paper.* P 13½.

1140	**354**	32p. multicoloured	.. .. ..	55	60

(Des Passmore Design. Litho Irish Security Stamp Ptg Ltd)

1997 (1 Oct). *Centenary of Publication of Bram Stoker's Dracula. T* **355** *and similar multicoloured designs. Chalk-surfaced paper.* P 14×15 (vert) or 15×14 (horiz).

1141	28p. Type **355**	.. ..	60	55
1142	32p. Dracula and female victim	..	65	60
1143	38p. Dracula emerging from coffin (horiz)	80	80
1144	52p. Dracula and wolf (horiz)	..	1·10	1·10
1141/4		Set of 4	2·75	2·75
MS1145	150×90 mm. As Nos. 1141/4. P 15		3·25	3·25

A second miniature sheet, 75×55 mm, containing No. 1142, was only available as a promotional item connected with the purchase of funsize bars of various Mars products or at face value from the Philatelic Bureau.

356 "The Nativity" (Kevin Kelly)

357 Christmas Tree

(Des Creative Inputs (Nos. 1146/8). Q. Design (No. 1149). Litho Irish Security Stamp Ptg Ltd)

1997 (18 Nov). *Christmas.* (a) *Stained Glass Windows. T* **356** *and similar vert designs. Multicoloured. Chalk-surfaced paper.* P 14×15.

1146	28p. Type **356**	.. ..	55	55
1147	32p. "The Nativity" (Sarah Purser and A. E. Child)	..	60	65
1148	52p. "The Nativity" (A. E. Child)	..	95	1·10
1146/8	.. .. ..	Set of 3	1·90	2·10

(b) *Self-adhesive booklet stamp.* P 9×10

1149	28p. Type **357**	.. ..	50	55
	a. Booklet pane. No. 1149×20	..	10·00	

No. 1149 as only available from £5.32 stamp booklets.

ÉIRE 32

358 Holding Heart

359 Lady Mary Heath and Avro Avian over Pyramids

(Des B. Asprey. Litho Irish Security Stamp Ptg Ltd)

1998 (26 Jan). *Greetings Stamps* (1st series). *T* **358** *and similar vert designs based on the "love is..." cartoon characters of Kim Casali. Multicoloured. Chalk-surfaced paper.* P 14×15.

1150	32p. Type **358**	.. ..	60	75
	a. Booklet pane. Nos. 1150/3	..	2·25	
1151	32p. Receiving letter	.. ..	60	75
1152	32p. Sitting on log	.. ..	60	75
1153	32p. With birthday presents	..	60	75
1150/3	.. ..	Set of 4	2·25	2·75

Nos. 1151/3 were only available from £2.56 stamp booklets containing two examples of No. 1150a. This pane exists in two different forms with either No. 1150 at right and No. 1153 at left or No. 1152 at right and No. 1151 at left. In each instance the right-hand stamp is imperforate at right. No. 1150 is available from both sheets and booklets.

For 30p values in these designs see Nos. 1173/6.

(Des B. Asprey. Litho Irish Security Stamp Ptg Ltd)

1998 (26 Jan). *Chinese New Year* ("Year of the Tiger"). *Chalk-surfaced paper.* P 14×15.

MS1154	124×73 mm. As Nos. 1151/3	..	2·25	2·50

The example of No. 1152 in No. **MS**1154 is imperforate at right.

(Des V. Killowry. Litho Irish Security Stamp Ptg Ltd)

1998 (24 Feb). *Pioneers of Irish Aviation. T* **359** *and similar horiz designs. Multicoloured. Chalk-surfaced paper.* P 15×14.

1155	28p. Type **359**	.. ..	60	55
	a. Booklet pane. Nos. 1155/8	..	3·00	
	b. Booklet pane. Nos. 1155/6 each × 2	3·00	
1156	32p. Col. James Fitzmaurice and Junkers W. 33 *Bremen* over Labrador	65	60
	a. Booklet pane. Nos. 1156×2 and 1157	3·00	
	b. Booklet pane. No. 1156 and 1158×2	3·00	
1157	44p. Captain J. P. Saul and Fokker FVIIa/3m *Southern Cross*	..	1·00	1·00
1158	52p. Captain Charles Blair and Sikorsky V-s 44 (flying boat)	..	1·25	1·25
1155/8	.. ..	Set of 4	3·25	3·00

Booklet panes Nos. 1155b and 1156a/b have margins all round. On No. 1155a there are margins on three sides, but the two right-hand stamps (Nos. 1156 and 1158) are each imperforate at right.

360 Show-jumping

(Des P. Curling. Litho Irish Security Stamp Ptg Ltd)

1998 (2 Apr). *Equestrian Sports.* T **360** *and similar multi-coloured designs. Chalk-surfaced paper.* P 14×15 (45p.) *or* 15×14 (*others*).

1159	30p. Type **360**	.. ..	70	60
1160	32p. Three-day eventing ..	.. ..	75	65
1161	40p. Gymkhana ..	.. ..	90	1·00
1162	45p. Dressage (*vert*)	.. ..	90	1·10
1159/62	.. .. ..	*Set of* 4	3·00	3·00
MS1163	126×84 mm. Nos. 1159/62	.. ..	3·00	3·00

361 Figure of "Liberty"

(Des R. Ballagh. Litho Irish Security Stamp Printing Ltd)

1998 (6 May). *Bicentenary of United Irish Rebellion.* T **361** *and similar horiz designs. Multicoloured. Chalk-surfaced paper.* P 15×14.

1164	30p. Type **361**	.. .. ..	75	80
	a. Horiz strip of 3. Nos. 1164/6	..	2·00	
1165	30p. United Irishman	.. ..	75	80
1166	30p. French soldiers	.. ..	75	80
1167	45p. Wolfe Tone ..	.. ..	1·00	1·25
	a. Horiz pair. Nos. 1167/8	..	2·00	2·50
1168	45p. Henry Joy McCracken	..	1·00	1·25
1164/8	.. .. ..	*Set of* 5	3·75	4·50

Nos. 1164/6 and 1167/8 were each printed together, horizontally *se-tenant,* in strips of 3 (30p.) or in pairs (45p.) throughout sheets of 12.

362 Gathering of the Boats, Kinvara

(Des J. Dunne. Litho Irish Security Stamp Ptg Ltd)

1998 (6 May). *Europa. Festivals.* T **362** *and similar horiz design. Multicoloured.* (*a*) P 15×14

1169	30p. Type **362**	.. ..	70	80
1170	40p. Puck Fair, Killorglin	..	80	95

(*b*) *Self-adhesive. Chalk-surfaced paper.* P 9½

1171	30p. Type **362**	.. ..	65	70
1172	30p. Puck Fair, Killorglin	..	65	70

Nos. 1169/70 were each issued in sheetlets of 10 (2×5) with enlarged illustrated left margins.

Nos. 1171/2, which are smaller 34×23 mm, occur in rolls of 100 with the surplus self-adhesive paper retained.

1998 (6 May). *Greetings Stamps (2nd series). Vert designs as Nos.* 1150/3, *but with changed face value. Multicoloured. Chalk-surfaced paper.* P 14×15.

1173	30p. As No. 1153	.. ..	70	80
	a. Booklet pane. Nos. 1173/6 ..		2·50	
1174	30p. As No. 1152	.. ..	70	80
1175	30p. As No. 1151	.. ..	70	80
1176	30p. Type **358**	.. ..	70	80
1173/6	.. .. ..	*Set of* 4	2·50	3·00

Nos. 1173/6 were only available from £2.40 stamp booklets containing two examples of No. 1173a. This pane exists in two different forms with either No. 1176 at right and No. 1173 at left or No. 1174 at right and No. 1175 at left. In each instance the right-hand stamp is imperforate at right.

363 Cyclists rounding Bend

(Des C. Harrison. Litho Irish Security Stamp Ptg Ltd)

1998 (2 June). *Visit of "Tour de France" Cycle Race to Ireland.* T **363** *and similar horiz designs. Multicoloured. Chalk-surfaced paper.* P 15×14.

1177	30p. Type **363**	.. ..	70	70
	a. Horiz strip of 4. Nos. 1177/80		2·50	
1178	30p. Two cyclists ascending hill ..	..	70	70
1179	30p. "Green jersey" cyclist and other competitor	.. ..	70	70
1180	30p. "Yellow jersey" (race leader)	..	70	70
1177/80	.. .. ..	*Set of* 4	2·50	2·50

Nos. 1177/80 were printed together, *se-tenant,* in horizontal strips of 4 throughout the sheet.

364 Voter and Local Councillors of 1898

365 *Asgard II* (cadet brigantine)

(Des J. Dunne. Litho Irish Security Stamp Ptg Ltd)

1998 (2 June). *Democracy Anniversaries.* T **364** *and similar horiz designs. Multicoloured. Chalk-surfaced paper.* P 15×14.

1181	30p. Type **364** (Cent of Local Government (Ireland) Act)	.. ..	60	60
1182	32p. European Union flag and harp symbol (25th anniv of Ireland's entry into European Community)		65	65
1183	35p. Woman voter and suffragettes, 1898 (Cent of women's right to vote in local elections)	.. ..	75	75
1184	45p. Irish Republic flag (50th anniv of Republic of Ireland Act)	..	1·00	1·00
1181/4	.. .. ..	*Set of* 4	2·75	2·75

(Des FOR Design. Litho Irish Security Stamp Ptg Ltd)

1998 (20 July). *Cutty Sark International Tall Ships Race, Dublin.* T **365** *and similar multicoloured designs. Chalk-surfaced paper.*

(*a*) P 14×15 (30p.) *or* 15×14 (45p, £1)

1185	30p. Type **365**	.. ..	55	60
	a. Pair. Nos. 1185/6	..	1·10	1·25
	b. Perf 15	.. ..	55	60
	ba. Booklet pane. Nos. 1185b×2 and 1186b with margins all round		1·65	
1186	30p. U.S.C.G. *Eagle* (cadet barque)	..	55	60
	b. Perf 15	..	55	60
	ba. Booklet pane. Nos. 1186b/8b with margins all round		1·10	
1187	45p. *Boa Esperanza* (caravel) (*horiz*)	..	80	85
	b. Perf 15	..	80	85
1188	£1 *Royalist* (training brigantine) (*horiz*)		1·75	1·90
	b. Perf 15	.. ..	1·75	1·90
1185/8	.. .. ..	*Set of* 4	3·50	3·75

(b) Self-adhesive. P 9¹/₂

1189	30p.	Boa Esperanza (horiz)	..	..	55	60
		a. Strip of 4. Nos. 1189/92	..	..	2·10	
1190	30p.	Type 365	..	..	55	60
1191	30p.	U.S.C.G. Eagle	..	..	55	60
1192	30p.	Royalist (horiz)	..	..	55	60
1189/92		..	..	Set of 4	2·10	2·25

Nos. 1185b/8b were only available from £2.65 stamp booklets.
Nos. 1189/92 are smaller, 34×23 or 23×34 mm, and occur, se-tenant, in strips of 4 or rolls of 100 with the surplus self-adhesive paper around each stamp retained.
Nos. 1185ba and 1186ba also exist overprinted for "Stampa 98".

366 Ashworth Pillarbox (1856)

367 Mary Immaculate College, Limerick

(Des M. Craig. Litho Irish Security Stamp Ptg Ltd)

1998 (3 Sept). *Irish Postboxes. T **366** and similar vert designs. Multicoloured. Chalk-surfaced paper. P 15×14.*

1193	30p.	Type 366	..	..	55	60
		a. Horiz strip of 4. Nos. 1193/6		..	2·10	
1194	30p.	Irish Free State wallbox (1922)	..	55	60
1195	30p.	Double pillarbox (1899)	..	55	60
1196	30p.	Penfold pillarbox (1866)	..	55	60
1193/6		..	..	Set of 4	2·10	2·40

Nos. 1193/6 were printed together, se-tenant, in horizontal strips of 4 throughout the sheet of 12.

(Des J. McPartlin (45p), E. Patton (others). Litho Irish Security Stamp Ptg Ltd)

1998 (3 Sept). *Anniversaries. T **367** and similar multicoloured designs. Chalk-surfaced paper. P 14×15 (40p.) or 15×14 (others).*

1197	30p.	Type 367 (centenary)	..	55	60
1198	40p.	Newtown School, Waterford (bicent) (vert)	..	70	75
1199	45p.	Trumpeters (50th anniv of Universal Declaration of Human Rights)	..	80	85
1197/9		..	.. Set of 3	2·00	2·10

(Des FOR Design. Litho Security Stamp Ptg Ltd)

1998 (4 Sept). *"Portugal '98" International Stamp Exhibition, Lisbon. Sheet, 101×71 mm, containing design as No. 1187. Chalk-surfaced paper. P 15×14.*

MS1200 £2 Boa Esperanza (caravel) (horiz) .. 3·50 3·75

368 Cheetah

(Des F. O'Conner. Litho Walsall)

1998 (8 Oct). *Endangered Animals. T **368** and similar multicoloured designs. P 14.*

1201	30p.	Type 368	..	..	55	60
		a. Horiz pair. Nos. 1201/2	..	1·10	1·25	
1202	30p.	Scimitar-horned Oryx	..	55	60	
1203	40p.	Golden Lion Tamarin (vert)	..	70	75	
1204	45p.	Tiger (vert)	..	..	80	85
1201/4		..	..	Set of 4	2·50	2·75
MS1205	150×90 mm. As Nos. 1201/4. P 15		..	2·50	2·75	

Nos. 1201/4 were printed together, se-tenant, in horizontal pairs throughout the sheet.
No. MS1205 also exists with an enlarged top margin overprinted for "Stampa '98" National Stamp Exhibition, Dublin.

369 The Holy Family   **370** Choir Boys

(Des P. Lynch (Nos. 1206/8), J. Laffan (No. 1209))

1998 (17 Nov). *Christmas. (a) Litho Irish Security Stamp Ptg Ltd. T **369** and similar vert designs. Multicoloured. Chalk-surfaced paper. P 14×15.*

1206	30p.	Type 369	..	..	55	60
1207	32p.	Shepherds	..	..	60	65
1208	45p.	Three Kings	..	..	80	85
1206/8		..	..	Set of 3	1·90	2·10

(b) Litho SNP Cambec, Australia. Self-adhesive. Phosphor frame. P 11¹/₂

1209	30p.	Type 370	..	..	55	60
		a. Booklet pane. No. 1209×20	..	10·00	

No. 1209, on which the phosphor frame appears greenish yellow under U.V. light, was only available from £5.40 stamp booklets.

371 Puppy and Heart   **372** Micheál Mac Liammóir

(Des M. Connor. Litho Irish Security Stamp Ptg Ltd)

1999 (26 Jan). *Greetings Stamps. Pets. T **371** and similar vert designs. Multicoloured. Chalk-surfaced paper. Phosphor frame. P 14×15.*

1210	30p.	Type 371	..	..	55	60
		a. Booklet pane. Nos. 1210/13	..	2·10	
1211	30p.	Kitten and ball of wool	..	55	60
1212	30p.	Goldfish	..	..	55	60
1213	30p.	Rabbit with lettuce leaf	..	55	60
1210/13		..	..	Set of 4	2·10	2·40

Nos. 1211/13, on which the phosphor appears green under U.V. light, were only available from £2.40 stamp booklets containing two examples of No. 1210a. This pane exists in two different forms with either No. 1210 at left and No. 1213 at right or No. 1213 at left and No. 1210 at right. In each instance the right-hand stamp is imperforate at right. No. 1210 is available from both sheets and booklets.

(Des M. Connor. Litho Irish Security Stamp Ptg Ltd)

1999 (26 Jan). *Chinese New Year ("Year of the Rabbit").*
Chalk-surfaced paper. Phosphor frame. P 14×15.
MS1214 124×74 mm. Nos. 1211/13 .. 1·60 1·75
The example of No. 1213 is imperforate at right.

(Des Creative Inputs. Litho Irish Security Stamp Ptg Ltd)

1999 (16 Feb). *Irish Actors and Actresses. T* **372** *and similar*
vert designs. Chalk-surfaced paper. Phosphor frame. P 14×15.
1215 30p. black and yellow-brown 55 60
1216 45p. black and bright green 80 85
1217 50p. black and ultramarine 90 95
1215/17 .. .. *Set of* 3 2·25 2·40
Designs: 45p. Siobhán McKenna; 50p. Noel Purcell.

373 Irish Emigrant Ship   374 *Polly Woodside* (barque)

(Des H. Paine and T. Mann. Litho Irish Security Stamp Ptg Ltd)

1999 (26 Feb). *Ireland—U.S.A. Joint Issue. Irish Emigration.*
Chalk-surfaced paper. Phosphor frame. P 15×14.
1218 **373** 45p. multicoloured 80 85
A stamp in a similar design was issued by the U.S.A.

(Des V. Killowry. Litho Walsall)

1999 (19 Mar). *Maritime Heritage. T* **374** *and similar*
multicoloured designs. Chalk-surfaced paper. Phosphor frame.
P 14.
1219 30p. Type **374** 55 60
1220 35p. *Ilen* (schooner) 65 70
1221 45p. R.N.L.I. Cromer class lifeboat (*horiz*).. 80 85
1222 £1 Titanic (*liner*) (*horiz*) .. .. 1·75 1·90
1219/22 .. .. *Set of* 4 3·75 4·00
MS1223 150×90 mm. No. 1222×2. No phosphor
frame .. .. 3·50 3·75
On Nos. 1219/23, the phosphor shows green under U.V. light.
No. **MS**1223 also exists overprinted with the "Australia '99",
International Stamp Exhibition, Melbourne, logo in gold.

(Litho SNP Ausprint)

1999 (19 Mar). *Ireland—Australia Joint Issue.* Polly Woodside
(*barque*). *Sheet* 137×72 *mm. Multicoloured. Phosphorised*
paper. P 14×14¹/₂.
MS1224 45 c. Type **603** of Australia; 30p. Type **374**
(*No.* **MS**1224 *was sold at* 52p. *in Ireland*) .. 95 1·00
No. **MS**1224 includes the "Australia '99" emblem on the sheet
margin and was postally valid in Ireland to the value of 30p. The
same miniature sheet was also available in Australia.

375 Sean Lemass   376 European Currency Emblem

(Des Creative Inputs. Litho Irish Security Stamp Ptg Ltd)

1999 (29 Apr). *Birth Centenary of Sean Lemass (politician).*
Chalk-surfaced paper. Phosphor frame. P 14×15.
1225 **375** 30p. black and deep bluish green .. 55 60

(Des Creative Inputs. Litho Irish Security Stamp Ptg Ltd)

1999 (29 Apr). *Introduction of Single European Currency.*
Chalk-surfaced paper. Phosphor frame. P 15×14.
1226 **376** 30p. multicoloured 55 60
The face value of No. 1226 is shown in both Irish and Euro
currency.

377 European Flags   378 Swans, Kilcolman Nature
Reserve

(Des J. McPartlin. Litho Irish Security Stamp Ptg Ltd)

1999 (29 Apr). *50th Anniv of Council of Europe. Chalk-surfaced*
paper. Phosphor frame. P 14×15.
1227 **377** 45p. multicoloured 80 85

(Des F. O'Connor. Litho Irish Security Stamp Ptg Ltd)

1999 (29 Apr). *Europa. Parks and Gardens. T* **378** *and similar*
horiz design. Chalk-surfaced paper. Phosphor frame.

(a) P 15×14.
1228 30p. Type **378** 55 60
1229 40p. Fallow Deer, Phoenix Park .. 70 75

(b) Self-adhesive. P 9.
1230 30p. Type **378** 55 60
1231 30p. Fallow Deer, Phoenix Park .. 55 60
1228/31 .. .. *Set of* 4 2·25 2·50
Nos. 1228/9 were each issued in sheets of 10 (2×5) with
enlarged illustrated left margins.
Nos. 1230/1, which are smaller, 34×23 mm., were only
available in rolls of 100 on which the surplus self-adhesive paper
was retained.

379 Father James Cullen   380 Elderly Man and Child
and St. Francis Xavier   using Computer
Church, Dublin

(Des Creative Inputs. Litho Irish Security Stamp Ptg Ltd)

1999 (15 June). *Centenary of Pioneer Total Abstinence*
Association. Chalk-surfaced paper. Phosphor frame. P 14×15.
1232 **379** 32p. olive-brown, bistre and black .. 60 65

(Des C. Harrison. Litho Irish Security Stamp Ptg Ltd)

1999 (15 June). *International Year of Older Persons. Chalk-surfaced paper. Phosphor frame. P 15×14.*
1233 **380** 30p. multicoloured 55 60

1874 - 1999
125 Years of the Universal Postal Union

Éire   30

381 Postal Van, 1922

(Des Creative Inputs. Litho Irish Security Stamp Ptg Ltd)

1999 (15 June). *125th Anniv of Universal Postal Union. T 381 and similar horiz design. Chalk-surfaced paper. Phosphor frame. P 15×14.*
1234 30p. grey-green and slate-green .. 55 60
   a. Pair. Nos. 1234/5 .. .. 1·10
1235 30p. multicoloured 55 60
Designs:— No. 1234, Type **381**; No. 1235, Modern postal lorries.
Nos. 1234/5 were printed together, *se-tenant*, in horizontal or vertical pairs throughout sheets of 16.

éIRE   30

Danno Keeffe

🏅 TEAM OF THE MILLENNIUM

382 Danno Keeffe

(Des F. O'Connor)

1999 (17 Aug). *Gaelic Athletic Association "Millennium Football Team". T 382 and similar horiz designs. Multicoloured. Phosphor frame. Chalk-surfaced paper.* (a) *Litho Irish Security Ptg Ltd. P 15×14.*
1236	30p. Type **382**		..		55	60
	a. Sheetlet. Nos. 1236/50 plus label				8·25	
1237	30p. Enda Colleran	..		..	55	60
1238	30p. Joe Keohane		..	..	55	60
1239	30p. Seán Flanagan	..	..	..	55	60
1240	30p. Seán Murphy	..		..	55	60
1241	30p. John Joe Reilly	..	..	..	55	60
1242	30p. Martin O'Connell		..	..	55	60
1243	30p. Mick O'Connell		..	..	55	60
1244	30p. Tommy Murphy			..	55	60
1245	30p. Seán Ó'Neill			..	55	60
1246	30p. Seán Purcell		..	..	55	60
1247	30p. Pat Spillane		..	..	55	60
1248	30p. Mikey Sheehy	..		..	55	60
1249	30p. Tom Langan	..		..	55	60
1250	30p. Kevin Heffernan		..	..	55	60
1236/50	.. ..			Set of 15	8·25	9·00

(b) *Self-adhesive booklet stamps. Litho SNP Ausprint, Australia. P 11½.*
1251	30p. Danno Keeffe	..	..	..	55	60
	a. Booklet pane. Nos. 1251, 1253, 1255, 1258, 1262×2 and 1263×2			..	4·25	
1252	30p. Enda Colleran		..	..	55	60
	a. Booklet pane. Nos. 1252, 1254, 1261 and 1264, each×2			..	4·25	
1253	30p. Joe Keohane	..	..	..	55	60
1254	30p. Seán Flanagan	..		..	55	60
1255	30p. Seán Murphy		..	..	55	60
1256	30p. John Joe Reilly	..		..	55	60
	a. Booklet pane. Nos. 1256 and 1260, each×4			..	4·25	
1257	30p. Martin O'Connell		..	..	55	60
	a. Booklet pane. Nos. 1257×3, 1259×2 and 1265×3			..	4·25	
1258	30p. Mick O'Connell	..		..	55	60
1259	30p. Tommy Murphy	..		..	55	60
1260	30p. Seán Ó'Neill	..		..	55	60
1261	30p. Seán Purcell	..		..	55	60
1262	30p. Pat Spillane	..		..	55	60
1263	30p. Mikey Sheehy	..		..	55	60
1264	30p. Tom Langan	..		..	55	60
1265	30p. Kevin Heffernan	..		..	55	60
1251/65	.. .. ..			Set of 15	8·25	9·00

Nos. 1236/50 were issued together, *se-tenant*, in sheetlets of 15 stamps and a label. No. 1236a also exists imperforate from a limited edition folder sold at £30.

Nos. 1251/65 are smaller, 33×23 mm, and were only issued in four different £2.40 stamp booklets in which the surplus self-adhesive paper around each stamp was retained.

STAMP BOOKLETS

Nos. SB1 to SB24 are stitched. Subsequent booklets have their panes attached by the selvedge, *unless otherwise stated.*

B 1 Harp and Monogram

B 2 Harp and "EIRE"

1931 (21 Aug)–**40.** *Black on red cover as Type* B **1.**
SB1   2s. booklet containing six ¹/₂d., six 2d. (Nos. 71, 74), each in block of 6, and nine 1d. (No. 72) in block of 6 and pane of 3 stamps and 3 labels (No. 72d or 72dw) .. .. *From* £1900
   Edition Nos.:—31–1, 31–2, 32–3, 33–4, 33–5, 34–6, 34–7, 35–8, 35–9, 36–10, 36–11, 37–12, 37–13, 37–14, 15–38, 16–38, 17–38,
   a. Cover as Type B 2
   Edition Nos.:—18–39, 19–39, 20–39, 21–40, 22–40

1940. *Black on red cover as Type* B **2.**
SB2   2s. booklet containing six ¹/₂d., six 2d. (Nos. 71, 74), each in block of 6, and nine 1d. (No. 72) in block of 6 and pane of 3 stamps and 3 labels (No. 112d or 112dw) £6500
   Edition No.:—22–40

1940. *Black on red cover as Type* B **2.**
SB3   2s. booklet containing six ¹/₂d., six 2d. (Nos. 111, 114), each in block of 6, and nine 1d. (No. 112) in block of 6 and pane of 3 stamps and 3 labels (No. 112d or 112dw) £6500
   Edition No.:—23–40

1941–44. *Black on red cover as Type* B **2.**
SB4   2s. booklet containing twelve ¹/₂d., six 1d. and six 2d. (Nos. 111/12, 114) in blocks of 6 ..   .. £750
   Edition Nos.:—24–41, 25–42, 26–44

B 3

1945. *Black on red cover as Type* B **3.**
SB5   2s. booklet containing twelve ¹/₂d., six 1d. and six 2d. (Nos. 111/12, 114) in blocks of 6 ..   .. £650
   Edition No.:—27–45

1946. *Black on buff cover as Type* B **2.**
SB6   2s. booklet containing twelve ¹/₂d., six 1d. and six 2d. (Nos. 111/12, 114) in blocks of 6 ..   .. £475
   Edition No.:—28–46

1946–47. *Black on buff cover as Type* B **2.**
SB7   2s. booklet containing twelve ¹/₂d., six 1d. and six 2d. (Nos. 133, 112, 114) in blocks of 6 .. *From* £225
   Edition Nos.:—29–46, 30–47

B 4 Harp only

1948–50. *Black on red cover as Type* B **4.**
SB8   2s. 6d. booklet containing six ¹/₂d., twelve 1d. and six 2¹/₂d. (Nos. 133, 112, 115) in blocks of 6 .. £120
   Edition Nos.:—31–48, 32–49, 33–50

1951–53. *Black on buff cover as Type* B **4.**
SB9   2s. 6d. booklet containing six ¹/₂d., twelve 1d. and six 2¹/₂d. (Nos. 133, 112, 115) in blocks of 6 .. 55·00
   Edition Nos.:—34–51, 35–52, 36–53

1954 (24 Nov). *Black on buff cover as Type* B **4.**
SB10   4s. booklet containing six ¹/₂d., six 1¹/₂d. and twelve 3d. (Nos. 133, 113, 116) in blocks of 6   £110
   Edition No.:—37–54

1956 (17 Dec). *Black on buff cover as Type* B **4.**
SB11   4s. booklet containing twelve 1d. and twelve 3d. (Nos. 112, 116) in blocks of 6   ..   .. 60·00
   Edition No.:—38–56

B 5

1958–61. *Black on buff cover as Type* B **5.**
SB12   4s. booklet containing twelve 1d. and twelve 3d. (Nos. 112, 116) in blocks of 6   ..   .. 60·00
   Edition Nos.:—39–58, 40–59, 41–60, 42–61

1962 (23 Oct)–**63.** *Black on buff cover as Type* B **5.**
SB13   3s. booklet containing six 2d. and six 4d. (Nos. 114, 117) in blocks of 6   ..   .. *From* 55·00
   Edition Nos.:—43–62, 44–63 (June)

B **6**

1964 (Sept). *Red on yellow cover as Type* B **6**.
SB14   3s. booklet containing twelve 1d. and six 4d. (Nos.
        112, 117) in blocks of 6   ..   ..   .. 35·00

B **7**

1966 (1–9 Dec). *Covers as Type* B **7** *in red* (*No.* SB15), *blue* (*No.*
SB16) *or green* (*No* SB17).
SB15   2s. 6d. booklet containing six 2d. and six 3d. (Nos.
        114, 116) in blocks of 6 (9 Dec)   ..   .. 20·00
SB16   2s. 6d. booklet containing six 5d. (No. 228) in
        block of 6 (9 Dec)   ..   ..   .. 15·00
SB17   5s. booklet containing twelve 5d. (No. 228) in
        blocks of 6   ..   .. 30·00

B **8**

1969 (12 Sept). *Plain blue-green cover as Type* B **8**.
SB18   6s. booklet containing twelve 6d. (No. 253) in
        blocks of six ..   .. 40·00

1971 (15 Feb). *Plain slate-green cover as Type* B **8**.
SB19   30p. booklet containing six ½p., twelve 1p. and
        six 2½p. in panes of 6 (Nos. 287ab or
        287awb, 288ca or 288cwa, 291ba or 291bwa) 32·00

1974 (11 Mar). *Green cover as Type* B **8**.
SB20   50p. booklet containing ten 5p. in panes of 5
        stamps and 1 label (No. 295ad or 295adw)   24·00

1974 (11 Mar). *Blue cover as Type* B **8**.
SB21   50p. booklet containing five 1p. in pane of 5
        stamps and 1 label (Nos. 288cb or 288cwb),
        six 2½p. and six 5p. in panes of 6 (Nos.
        291ba or 291bwa, 295ae or 295awe)   .. 11·00

1975 (27 Jan). *Covers as Type* B **8**, *in rose* (*No.* SB22) *or light
grey* (*No.* SB23).
SB22   40p. booklet containing five 1p., 2p. and 5p. each
        in panes of 5 stamps and 1 label (Nos. 288cb
        or 288cwb, 290ba or 290bwa, 295ad or
        295awd)   ..   .. 3·50
SB23   70p. booklet containing ten 2p. and 5p. each in
        panes of 5 stamps and 1 label (Nos. 290ba or
        290bwa, 295ad or 295awd)   ..   .. 4·50

1977 (21 Mar). *Yellow-olive cover similar to Type* B **8**.
SB24   50p. booklet containing five 1p., 2p. and 7p. each
        in panes of 5 stamps and 1 label (Nos. 288cb
        or 288cwb, 290ba or 290bwa, 348a)   .. 10·00

Stampai/Postage Stamps

B **9**   Four Courts

1983 (15 Aug). *Yellow-green cover as Type* B **9**.
SB25   £1 booklet containing *se-tenant* pane of 7 stamps
        and 1 label (No. 535a)   ..   .. 2·50
   No. SB25 was an experimental issue available from two
machines, accepting two 50p. coins, at the G.P.O. Dublin, and
from the Philatelic Bureau.

B **10**

1984 (9 July). *Dull green, greenish yellow and black cover as
Type* B **10**.
SB26   £2 booklet containing *se-tenant* pane of 12 (No.
        535ba)   ..   .. 6·50
   No. SB26 actually contains £2.26 worth of stamps, but was
sold at a discount of 26p. by the Irish Post Office from 9 July
until 10 August.

Stampai

B **11**   Custom House, Dublin, in 19th Century

1985 (27 June). *Yellowish green cover as Type* B **11**.
SB27   £1 booklet containing *se-tenant* pane of 6 (No.
        533ab)   ..   .. 5·50

B **12**

1985 (27 June). *Bright green cover as Type* B **12**.
SB28   £2 booklet containing *se-tenant* pane of 12 (No.
        533ac)   ..   .. 9·00

B 13

1986 (8 Sept). *Black, light green and pale yellow cover as Type* B **13**.
SB29 £2 booklet containing *se-tenant* pane of 12 (No. 533ad) .. .. 9·00

B **14** Custom House, Dublin
(*Illustration further reduced. Actual size 137×70 mm*)

1988 (1 Mar). *Dublin Millenium. Multicoloured cover as Type* B **14**.
SB30 £2.24, booklet containing eight 24p. in panes of 4 (No. 688a) (one inscr in Irish, one in English) 7·00
No. SB30 also exists with the booklet cover overprinted for "SPRING STAMPEX 1988", "7 Internationale Briefmarken-Messe" (Essen), "FINLANDIA 88" and "SYDPEX 88" exhibitions.

1988 (24 Nov). *Maroon and black cover as Type* B **11**, *but showing Courthouse, Cork.*
SB31 £2 booklet containing *se-tenant* pane of 12 (No. 533ae) .. .. 10·00

B **15** Gordon Bennett Race, 1903
(*Illustration further reduced. Actual size 132×60 mm*)

1989 (11 Apr). *Irish Motoring Classics. Multicoloured cover as Type* B **15**.
SB32 £2.41, booklet containing two different *se-tenant* panes of 4 (Nos. 718a/b) .. .. .. 6·50

B **16** 8th-century Gilt-silver Brooch
(*Illustration further reduced. Actual size 160×100 mm*)

1989 (15 June). 1300th *Death Anniv of Saints Kilian, Totnan and Colman. Multicoloured cover as Type* B **16**. *Stitched.*
SB33 £4.48, booklet containing sixteen 28p. in panes of 4 (No. 726a) .. .. 11·00
No. SB33 exists overprinted for "PHILEXFRANCE 89" or "WORLD STAMP EXPO '89".

B **17** (*Illustration further reduced. Actual size 136×74 mm*)

1990 (22 Mar). *Greetings Booklet. Multicoloured cover as Type* B **17**. *Stitched.*
SB34 £1.98, booklet containing two *se-tenant* panes of 4 (No. 766a) and eight greetings labels 15·00
No. SB34 was sold at £1.98, providing a discount of 26p. off the face value of the stamps.

B **18** (*Illustration further reduced. Actual size 161×99 mm*)

1990 (3 May). 150th *Anniv of the Penny Black. Multicoloured cover as Type* B **18**. *Stitched.*
SB35 £6 booklet containing *se-tenant* panes of 8, 4 and 5 (Nos. 535ca, 547ba/bb and pane of 4 (No. 774a) 50·00
No. SB25 exists overprinted for "Stamp World London 90" exhibition.

B **19** Garden at Powerscourt, Co. Wicklow
(*Illustration further reduced. Actual size 150×75 mm*)

1990 (30 Aug). *Garden Flowers. Multicoloured cover as Type* B **19**. *Stitched.*
SB36 £2.59, booklet containing two different *se-tenant* panes of 4 (Nos. 781a/b) .. .. .. 10·00

B **20** 7th-century Tara Brooch

1990 (15 Nov). *Irish Heritage. Black and bright blue cover as Type* B **20**.
SB37   £1 booklet containing *se-tenant* pane of 7 stamps and 1 label (No. 747ab) .. .. .. 3·00

B **21**   View of Dublin
(Illustration further reduced. Actual size 140×85 *mm)*

1991 (11 Apr). *"Dublin* 1991 *European City of Culture". Multicoloured cover as Type* B **21**.
SB38   £2.60, booklet containing two different *se-tenant* panes of 3 (Nos. 800a/b) .. .. .. 8·50

B **22**   Ardagh Chalice

1991 (14 May)–**92**. *Covers as Type* B **22**.
SB39   £1 booklet containing *se-tenant* pane of 5 stamps and 1 label (No. 808a) (black and green cover as Type B **22**) .. .. .. 1·75
SB40   £1 booklet containing *se-tenant* pane of 5 stamps and 1 label (No. 808a) (black and orange-yellow cover showing St. Patrick's Bell Shrine) (25.2.92) .. .. .. 1·75

B **23** *(Illustration further reduced. Actual size* 161×99 *mm)*

1991 (17 Oct). *Fishing Fleet. Multicoloured cover as Type* B **23**. *Stitched.*
SB41   £5 booklet containing *se-tenant* panes of 5 and 7 and 1 label (Nos. 747ac, 748ba) and two different *se-tenant* panes of 4 (Nos. 819a/b)   20·00

B **24** *(Illustration further reduced. Actual size* 138×75 *mm)*

1992 (2 Apr). *Greetings Booklet. Multicoloured cover as Type* B **24**. *Stitched.*
SB42   £2.40, booklet containing two *se-tenant* panes of 4 (No. 840a) and eight greetings labels .. 10·00

B **25** *(Illustration further reduced. Actual size* 161×100 *mm)*

1992 (15 Oct). *Single European Market. Deep bluish violet and greenish yellow cover as Type* B **25**. *Stitched.*
SB43   £4.80, booklet containing fifteen 32p. in three panes of 4 (No. 856a) and one pane of 3 (No. 856b) .. .. 11·00

B **26**   "Banks of the Seine, near Paris" (N. Hone)
(Illustration further reduced. Actual size 161×100 *mm)*

1993 (4 Mar). *Irish Impressionist Painters. Multicoloured cover as Type* B **26**. *Stitched.*
SB44   £4.68, booklet containing four *se-tenant* panes (Nos. 867a×2, 867b and 869a) .. .. 11·50

B **27**   Lismore Crozier

1993 (24 Sept)–**95**. *Covers as Type* B **27**.
SB45   £1 booklet containing *se-tenant* pane of 4 (No. 748ca) (bright greenish blue cover as Type B **27**) .. .. 1·75
SB46   £1 booklet containing *se-tenant* pane of 4 (No. 748cb) (black and bright vermilion cover showing enamelled latchet brooch) (2.3.94)   1·75
SB46*a*   £1 booklet containing *se-tenant* pane of 4 (No. 748cb) (black and bright orange-red cover showing Gleninsheen Collar) (28.2.95)   1·75
SB46*b*   £1 booklet containing *se-tenant* pane of 4 (No. 748a) (black and bright reddish violet cover showing Broighter Collar) (16.11.95) .. 1·75

B 28 Front and Side View of Dublin Bus Leyland Olympian
(*Illustration further reduced. Actual size* 131×61 *mm*)

1993 (12 Oct). *Irish Buses. Multicoloured cover as Type B 28. Stitched.*
SB47 £2.84, booklet containing two different *se-tenant* panes (Nos. 886a/b) .. .. 8·00

B 29 (*Illustration further reduced. Actual size* 138×75 *mm*)

1994 (27 Jan). *Greetings Booklet. Multicoloured cover as Type B 29. Stitched.*
SB48 £2.56, booklet containing two *se-tenant* panes of four 32p. (No. 896a) .. .. 8·50

B 30 (*Illustration further reduced. Actual size* 137×60 *mm*)

1994 (27 Apr). *Parliamentary Anniversaries. Multicoloured cover as Type B 30. Stitched.*
SB49 £1.92, booklet containing two different *se-tenant* panes (Nos. 908a/b) .. .. 7·00

B 31 (*Illustration further reduced. Actual size* 161×101 *mm*)

1994 (18 Oct). *Irish Nobel Prizewinners. Multicoloured cover as Type B 31. Stitched.*
SB50 £4.84, booklet containing four different *se-tenant* panes (Nos. 928b/d and 930a) .. .. 11·50

B 32 (*Illustration further reduced. Actual size* 138×75 *mm*)

1995 (24 Jan). *Greetings Booklet. Multicoloured cover as Type B 32. Stitched.*
SB51 £2.56, booklet containing two *se-tenant* panes of four 32p. (No. 936a) .. .. .. 8·50

B 33 Blessing before Battle
(*Illustration reduced. Actual size* 161×100 *mm*)

1995 (15 May). *Military Uniforms. Multicoloured cover as Type B 33. Stitched.*
SB52 £4.80, booklet containing four different *se-tenant* panes (Nos. 954a/d) .. .. 11·50

B 34 (*Illustration reduced. Actual size* 140×82 *mm*)

1995 (9 Oct). *Bicentenary of National Botanic Gardens, Glasnevin. Multicoloured cover as Type B 34. Stitched.*
SB53 £2.60, booklet containing two different *se-tenant* panes (Nos. 973a/b) .. .. 9·00

B 35 (*Illustration reduced. Actual size* 137 x 74 *mm*)

1996 (23 Jan). *Greetings Booklet. Multicoloured cover as Type B 35. Stitched.*
SB54 £2.56, booklet containing two *se-tenant* panes of four 32p. (No. 982a) .. .. 10·00

B **36** Steeplechasing
(Illustration reduced. Actual size 161×100 *mm)*

1996 (12 Mar). *Irish Horse Racing. Multicoloured cover as Type* B **36**. *Stitched.*
SB55   £4.92, booklet containing four different *se-tenant* panes (Nos. 991a, 992b/c and 993a)   .. 16·00

B **37** Coastal Patrol Vessel and Sailor
(Illustration reduced. Actual size 150×90 *mm)*

(Des Design Image)

1996 (18 July). 50*th Anniv of Irish Naval Service. Multicoloured cover as Type* B **37**. *Stitched.*
SB56   £2.24, booklet containing pane of three 32p. and pane of three values *se-tenant* (Nos. 1013a/b)   5·50

B **38** Farmyard Animals
(Illustration reduced. Actual size 137×73 *mm)*

1997 (28 Jan). *Greetings Booklet. Multicoloured cover as Type* B **38**. *Stitched.*
SB57   £2.56, booklet containing two *se-tenant* panes of four 32p. (No. 1100a)   ..   ..   .. 7·50

B **39** Robin

1997 (6 Mar). *Birds. Multicoloured cover as Type* B **39**. *Stamps attached by selvedge.*
SB58   £1 booklet containing pane of 4 (2×2) (No. 748bb)   ..   .. 1·75

B **40** The Baily Lighthouse
(Illustration reduced. Actual size 160×100 *mm)*

1997 (1 July). *Lighthouses. Multicoloured cover as Type* B **40**. *Stitched.*
SB59   £4.64, booklet containing four different, *se-tenant*, panes (Nos. 1136b/c, 1036da and 1038da)   ..   .. 10·00

B **41** Christmas Tree

1997 (18 Nov). *Christmas. Multicoloured cover as Type* B **41**. *Self-adhesive.*
SB60   £5.32, booklet containing pane of twenty 28p. (2×10) (No. 1149a) ..   .. 10·00
    No. SB60 was sold at £5.32 providing a discount of 28p. off the face value of the stamps.

1997 (6 Dec). *Multicoloured cover as Type* B **39** *showing Peregrine Falcon. Stamps attached by selvedge.*
SB61   £1 booklet containing pane of 4 (2×2) (No. 1080a)   ..   .. 1·75

NEW INFORMATION

The editor is always interested to correspond with people who have new information that will improve or correct the Catalogue.

B 42 On Swing
(Illustration further reduced. Actual size 138×74 mm)

1998 (26 Jan). *Greetings Booklet. Multicoloured cover as Type B **42**. Stitched.*
SB62   £2.56, booklet containing two different *se-tenant* panes of four 32p. (No. 1150a)   ..   6·50

B 43 Early Aeroplane and Map
(Illustration further reduced. Actual size 160×100 mm)

1998 (24 Feb). *Pioneers of Irish Aviation. Multicoloured cover as Type B **43**. Stitched.*
SB63 $5.20, booklet containing four different, *se-tenant*, panes (Nos. 1155a/b and 1156a/b)   11·00

B 44 Blackbird

1998 (2 Apr). *Multicoloured cover as Type B **44**. Stamps attached by selvedge.*
SB64   £1 booklet containing pane of 5 stamps and 1 label (No. 1081a)   ..   ..   1·75

1998 (6 May). *Greetings Booklet. Multicoloured cover as Type B **42**, but inscribed "LETTER POST" in green border at foot. Stitched.*
SB65   £2.40, booklet containing two different *se-tenant* panes of four 30p. (No. 1173a)   ..   5·00

B 45 *Asgard II* (cadet brigantine)
(illustration reduced. Actual size 138×89 mm)

1998 (20 July). Cutty Sark *International Tall Ships Race, Dublin. Multicoloured cover as Type B **45**. Stitched.*
SB66   £2.65, booklet containing two different *se-tenant* panes of 3 (Nos. 1185ba and 1186ba)   4·50

B 46 Blackbird

1998 (4 Sept)–**99**. *Multicoloured cover as Type B **46**. Stamps attached by selvedge.*
SB67   £3 booklet containing pane of 10 (5×2) 30p. stamps (No. 1038ab)   ..   ..   5·50
      a. Containing pane No. 1038ar (stamps with phosphor frames) (3.99)   ..   ..   5·50

B 47 Choir Boys

1998 (17 Nov). *Christmas. Multicoloured cover as Type B **47**. Self-adhesive.*
SB68   £5.40, booklet containing pane of twenty 30p. (5×4) (No. 1209a)   ..   ..   ..   10·00
No. SB68 was sold at £5.40 providing a discount of 60p. off the face value of the stamps.

B 48 Domestic Pets
(Illustration reduced. Actual size 139×73 mm)

MINIMUM PRICE

The minimum price quote is 10p which represents a handling charge rather than a basis for valuing common stamps. For further notes about prices see introductory pages.

1999 (26 Jan). *Greetings Booklet. Pets. Multicoloured cover as Type* B **48**. *Stitched.*
SB69   £2.40, booklet containing two different *se-tenant* panes of four 30p. (No. 1210a)   ..   ..   4·00

B **49** Goldcrest

1999 (16 Feb). *Multicoloured cover as Type* B **49**. *Stamps attached by selvedge.*
SB70   £1 booklet containing pane of 5 stamps and 1 label (No. 1081ba) ..   ..   1·75

![5 EUROPEAN AIRMAIL STAMPS — Dublin]

B **50** Dublin

1999 (30 June). *Multicoloured covers as Type* B **50**. *Stamps attached by selvedge.*
SB71   £1.60, booklet containing pane of five 32p. plus 5 airmail labels (No. 1053ae)   ..   ..   3·00
SB72   £1.80, booklet containing pane of four 45p. and 4 airmail labels (No. 1057ae) (cover showing ornamental garden)   ..   ..   ..   3·25

B **51** "the Kingdom"

1999 (17 Aug). *Gaelic Athletics Association "Millennium Football Team". Multicoloured covers as Type* B **51**. *Self-adhesive.*
SB73   £2.40, booklet containing pane of 8 stamps (No. 1251a) (*cover as Type* B **51**)   ..   ..   4·25
SB74   £2.40, booklet containing pane of 8 stamps (No. 1252a) (*cover inscr* "the West awake")   ..   4·25
SB75   £2.40, booklet containing pane of 8 stamps (No. 1256a) (*cover inscr* "ulster abú")   ..   ..   4·25
SB76   £2.40, booklet containing pane of 8 stamps (No. 1257a) (*cover inscr* "Kings of Leinster")   ..   4·25

POSTAGE DUE STAMPS

From 1922 to 1925 Great Britain postage due stamps in both script and block watermarks were used without overprint.

D 1	D 2		D 3

(Des Ruby McConnell. Typo Govt Printing Works, Dublin)

1925 (20 Feb). *W* **10.** *P* 14×15.

D1	D 1	½d. emerald-green	..	..	12·00	16·00
D2		1d. carmine	..	..	15·00	3·00
		a. Wmk sideways	..	..	£550	£225
		w. Wmk inverted	..	..	£225	30·00
D3		2d. deep green	..	..	28·00	5·50
		a. Wmk sideways	..	..	45·00	15·00
		w. Wmk inverted	..	..	70·00	23·00
D4		6d. plum	..	..	6·00	6·50
D1/4				*Set of* 4	55·00	28·00

1940–70. *W* **22.** *P* 14×15.

D 5	D 1	½d. emerald-green (1942)	..	..	35·00	22·00
		w. Wmk inverted	..	..	£225	£120
D 6		1d. carmine (1941)	..	..	1·25	70
		w. Wmk inverted	..	..	55·00	6·50
D 7		1½d. vermilion (1953)	..	..	1·75	6·50
		w. Wmk inverted	..	..	15·00	21·00
D 8		2d. deep green (1940)	..	..	2·75	70
		w. Wmk inverted	..	..	20·00	6·50
D 9		3d. blue (10.11.52)	..	..	2·25	2·75
		w. Wmk inverted	..	..	6·00	5·00
D10		5d. blue-violet (3.3.43)	..	..	4·50	3·00
		w. Wmk inverted	..	..	6·50	7·00
D11		6d. plum (21.3.60)	..	..	3·00	2·00
		a. Wmk sideways (1968)	..	..	70	85
D12		8d. orange (30.10.62)	..	..	8·50	8·00
		w. Wmk inverted	..	..	17·00	18·00
D13		10d. bright purple (27.1.65)	..	..	8·50	7·50
D14		1s. apple-green (10.2.69)	..	..	6·00	9·00
		a. Wmk sideways (1970)	..	..	65·00	8·50
D5/14				*Set of* 10	65·00	55·00

1971 (15 Feb). *As Nos. D5/14, but with values in decimal currency and colours changed. W* **22.** *P* 14 × 15.

D15	D 1	1p. sepia	..	..	30	60
		a. Wmk sideways	..	..	1·75	1·50
		w. Wmk inverted	..	..	1·00	1·50
D16		1½p. light emerald	..	..	50	1·50
D17		3p. stone	..	..	90	1·75
		w. Wmk inverted	..	..	1·25	2·00
D18		4p. orange	..	..	90	1·25
D19		5p. greenish blue	..	..	95	2·50
		w. Wmk inverted	..	..	2·00	3·00
D20		7p. bright yellow	..	..	40	3·50
		w. Wmk inverted	..	..	1·50	3·50
D21		8p. scarlet	..	..	40	2·50
D15/21				*Set of* 7	3·75	12·00

1978 (20 Mar). *As Nos. D17/19, but no wmk. Chalk-surfaced paper. P* 14×15.

D22	D 1	3p. stone	..	..	1·50	5·00
D23		4p. orange	..	..	6·00	8·00
D24		5p. greenish blue	..	..	1·50	4·00
D22/4				*Set of* 3	8·00	15·00

1980 (11 June)–**85.** *Photo. Chalk-surfaced paper. P* 15.

D25	D 2	1p. apple green	..	..	30	55
D26		2p. dull blue	..	..	30	55
D27		4p. myrtle-green	..	..	40	55
D28		6p. flesh	..	..	40	70
D29		8p. chalky blue	..	..	40	75
D30		18p. green	..	..	75	1·25
D31		20p. Indian red (22.8.85)	..	..	2·25	4·50
D32		24p. bright yellowish green	..	..	75	2·00
D33		30p. deep violet blue (22.8.85)	..	..	3·00	5·50
D34		50p. cerise (22.8.85)	..	..	3·75	6·50
D25/34				*Set of* 10	11·00	20·00

The 1p. to 18p. are on white paper and the 20p., 30p. and 50p. on cream. The 24p. value exists on both types of paper.

(Des Q Design. Litho Irish Security Stamp Ptg Ltd)

1988 (6 Oct). *Chalk-surfaced paper. P* 14 × 15.

D35	D 3	1p. black, orange-vermilion & lemon	10	10
D36		2p. black, orange-verm & purple-brn	10	10
D37		3p. black, orange-vermilion and plum	10	10
D38		4p. black, orange-vermilion & brt vio	10	10
D39		5p. black, orge-vermilion & royal blue	10	10
D40		17p. black, orange-verm & dp yell-grn	30	35
D41		20p. black, orange-verm & slate-bl	35	40
D42		24p. black, orange-verm & dp turq-grn	40	45
D43		30p. black, orange-vermilion & dp grey	50	55
D44		50p. black, orge-verm & brownish grey	90	95
D45		£1 black, orge-vermilion & bistre-brn	1·75	1·90
D35/45			*Set of* 11	4·50	5·00

From 20 September 1993 labels in the above style were used to indicate postage due charges in the Dublin 2 delivery area. They are dispensed by a Pitney/Bowes machine, in much the same way as a meter mark, and can show any face value between 1p. and I£99.99. Such labels are not normally postmarked. Labels with face values of 32p. and 50p. were sold to collectors by the Philatelic Bureau.

THOMOND AND LONG ISLAND

Labels inscribed "Principality of Thomond" appeared on the philatelic market in the early 1960s. Thomond is the name of a district in western Ireland. The area does not have its own administration or postal service and the labels were not recognised by the Department of Posts & Telegraphs, Dublin.

Local carriage labels were issued for Long Island, County Cork in April 1973; they were intended to cover the cost of taking mail from the island to the nearest mainland post office. A local service operated for a few weeks before it was suppressed by the Irish Post Office. As the stamps were not accepted for national or international mail they are not listed here.

FIRST DAY COVERS

The following list provides prices for complete sets of commemorative or special stamps used on First Day Covers. Up to No. 148 (1949 James Mangan) the prices quoted are for plain envelopes. Those for subsequent issues are for illustrated envelopes. Special pictorial postmarks were introduced from Nos. 365/6 (1974 Centenary of the U.P.U.) onwards.

Nos.	FDC Price.	Nos.	FDC Price.	Nos.	FDC Price.	Nos.	FDC Price.
89/91	£675	306	1·25	505/7	2·50	732	1·50
92	£800	307/8	1·25	508/9	1·25	733/6	5·50
93	£140	309/10	1·25	510/11	2·00	MS737	6·50
94/5	£200	311/12	2·00	512/13	1·25	738/41	4·50
96/7	£275	313/14	5·50	514/15	3·00	742/3	4·00
98	£140	315/16	1·25	516/19	3·50	744/5	2·75
105/6	9·00	317	1·25	520/3	5·00	766/9	11·00
107/8	38·00	318/19	1·25	524/7	5·00	770/1	4·50
109/10	18·00	320/2	1·25	528/9	2·00	772/3	3·50
126/7	32·00	323	1·25	530/1	1·50	774/5	3·50
128	17·00	MS324	13·00	552/3	1·25	776/7	3·50
129/30	28·00	325/6	2·50	554/5	2·50	778/80	4·00
131/2	28·00	327/8	2·50	556/7	6·00	781/4	5·50
133/4	£225	329	1·25	558/62	6·00	785/8	6·50
135	20·00	330/1	2·50	MS563	9·00	789/92	4·50
136/7	30·00	332/3	1·25	564/8	5·00	793/4	2·25
138/9	15·00	334/5	1·75	569/70	3·00	795/7	3·50
144/5	14·00	336	1·25	571/4	4·75	MS798	4·00
146/7	22·00	337/8	3·00	575/6	1·25	799	1·75
148	18·00	360/1	1·25	577/80	6·00	800/3	6·00
149/51	40·00	362	1·25	MS581	8·00	804/5	4·25
152/3	25·00	363/4	1·25	582/5	6·00	806/7	3·00
154/5	£125	365/6	1·25	586/7	2·00	811/13	4·00
156/7	30·00	367/8	1·25	588/9	3·50	814/15	2·00
158/9	8·00	369/70	2·50	590	1·00	816/18	6·00
160/1	9·00	371/2	3·00	591	1·25	819/22	6·00
162/3	18·00	373/4	2·25	592/4	2·75	827/30	5·00
164/5	19·00	375	1·25	595/6	2·00	831/2	2·25
166/7	9·00	376/7	1·25	597/8	2·25	833	1·00
168/9	30·00	378/81	2·00	599	1·00	834/5	3·50
170/1	11·00	382/3	1·25	600/2	2·50	MS836	6·00
172/3	24·00	384/6	1·25	603/4	1·75	837/8	3·75
174/5	23·00	387/8	1·75	605/8	4·00	839	1·00
176/7	8·00	389/90	1·25	609/12	7·50	840/3	4·50
178/9	16·00	391/4	2·25	613/14	6·50	844/5	4·00
180/1	5·50	MS395	10·00	615/17	6·00	846/7	4·00
182/3	30·00	396/7	2·25	618/20	4·50	848/51	5·00
184/5	12·00	398	1·25	621/2	1·50	852/5	6·50
186/8	8·00	399/400	1·40	623/5	4·00	856	1·00
189/90	4·50	401/3	1·25	626/9	7·50	857/60	5·00
191/2	3·00	404/5	1·25	630/1	2·25	861/4	4·00
193/4	3·25	406/7	2·00	632/4	3·50	865/6	1·75
195/6	6·00	408	1·25	635/6	6·00	867/70	5·00
197/8	3·75	409/10	2·00	637/8	4·00	871/4	6·00
199/200	7·00	411/12	1·25	639/41	4·25	MS875	7·50
201/2	6·50	413/15	2·50	642/3	2·00	876/7	2·00
203/4	7·00	416/18	1·40	644/5	4·00	878/9	2·50
205/6	4·00	419/20	1·40	646/50	5·25	880/1	2·75
207/8	4·50	421/4	3·25	651/3	3·00	882/5	4·00
209/10	7·00	425/7	2·00	654/5	2·50	886/9	5·00
211/12	6·00	428	1·25	656/7	2·75	890/3	4·00
213/20	25·00	429/32	1·75	658/61	5·50	894/5	1·75
221/2	1·25	433/5	1·75	MS662	8·00	896/9	4·00
223/4	3·00	436/7	1·25	663/6	5·00	MS900	5·50
225/6	1·25	438	1·25	667/8	6·00	901/4	5·00
229/30	1·75	439/40	1·25	669/72	6·00	905/6	3·00
231/2	1·50	441	1·25	673/6	5·25	MS907	3·25
233/4	1·25	442/5	3·75	677/80	3·50	908/9	2·25
235/6	1·25	446/8	1·75	681/3	3·00	910/13	5·00
237/8	1·25	449	1·25	684/5	2·00	914/17	5·00
239/40	2·00	450/2	2·50	686/7	3·00	MS918	5·00
241/2	1·25	453	1·25	688	1·25	919/22	5·00
243/4	1·25	454/5	1·25	689/90	3·00	923/7	6·00
245/6	1·25	456/7	2·00	691/3	3·25	928/31	3·75
263/4	1·25	458	1·25	694/5	3·50	932/5	3·75
265/6	1·25	459/60	2·00	696/7	3·50	936/9	4·00
267/8	2·75	461/4	3·00	698/700	3·00	MS940	3·00
269/70	1·25	MS465	4·00	701/4	4·00	941/4	6·00
271	1·75	466/8	1·50	705/6	2·50	MS945	6·50
272/3	1·25	469/70	1·25	707	1·25	946/7	3·00
274/5	1·25	471/3	1·50	708/11	3·75	MS948	3·25
276/8	3·75	474/7	2·50	712/13	2·00	949/52	5·00
279	1·25	491/2	1·25	714/17	4·00	953	1·00
280	1·25	493/6	2·50	718/21	4·00	954/8	5·50
281/4	14·00	497	1·25	722/3	3·50	959/60	2·75
285/6	1·75	498	1·25	724/5	2·00	961/4	4·00
302/3	2·50	499	1·25	726	1·25	965/8	5·00
304/5	1·25	500/4	4·00	727/31	6·00	969/72	5·00

Nos.	FDC Price.	Nos.	FDC Price.	Nos.	FDC Price.	Nos.	FDC Price.
973/5	4·00	**MS**1022	5·50	1146/8	2·50	**MS**1205	3·25
976/7	2·75	1023/6	3·75	1150/3	3·00	1206/9	3·25
978/81	3·75	1027/30	4·00	**MS**1154	3·00	1210	75
982/5	4·00	1100/3	4·00	1155/8	3·25	1210a	3·00
MS986	4·00	**MS**1104	3·00	1159/62	3·75	**MS**1214	2·25
987/90	3·25	1105/16 (4)	10·00	**MS**1163	3·75	1215/17	3·00
991/5	5·50	1118/21	4·00	1164/8	5·25	1218	1·10
996	1·25	**MS**1122	4·50	1169/72	4·00	1219/22	5·00
997/1000	5·00	1123	1·00	1173/6	3·75	**MS**1223	4·75
1001/2	2·00	1124/7	4·00	1177/80	3·25	**MS**1224	1·25
MS1003	3·25	1128/30	2·75	1181/4	3·50	1225/7	2·75
1004/7	5·50	**MS**1131	5·50	1185/8	4·75	1228/31	3·00
MS1008	2·50	1132/5	3·50	1189/92	3·50	1232/3	1·50
1009/12	4·25	1136/9	3·75	1193/6	3·00	1234/5	1·50
1013/15	4·00	1140	1·00	1197/9	2·75		
1016/17	1·50	1141/4	3·25	**MS**1200	4·25		
1018/21	4·50	**MS**1145	3·50	1201/4	3·25		

YEAR PACKS AND YEAR BOOKS

1975–76 Pack	........12·00	1985	Pack ....22·00		Book ....45·00	1996	Pack ....30·00
1977	Pack ....9·50	1986	Pack ....21·00	1992	Pack ....26·00		Book ....60·00
1978	Pack ....9·50	1987	Pack ....20·00		Book ....40·00	1997	Pack ....28·00
1979	Pack ....8·00	1988	Pack ....22·00	1993	Pack ....23·00		Book ....40·00
1980	Pack ....7·00	1989	Pack ....24·00		Book ....45·00	1998	Pack ....32·00
1981	Pack ....15·00		Book ....50·00	1994	Pack ....26·00		Book ....40·00
1982	Pack ....13·00	1990	Pack ....25·00		Book ....42·00		
1983	Pack ....22·00		Book ....50·00	1995	Pack ....32·00		
1984	Pack ....19·00	1991	Pack ....25·00		Book ....42·00		

Commonwealth Collections

A choice of two expertly designed collections provides the perfect introduction for British Commonwealth enthusiasts. Each collection comprises over 400 of the highest quality stamps, elegant printed albums in which to display your collection plus three free gifts to assist you.

King George VI Collection (1936 - 1953)

A superb four volume rich red buckram album accompanies the collection of unmounted mint material. Produced in a loose-leaf format, it contains the finest quality illustrated leaves and comes complete with a specially prepared mount pack.

King George VI Only £750 or 5 payments of £150
(Retail value £884)

King George VI includes four loose-leaf albums, mount pack and over 400 unmounted mint stamps.

Queen Elizabeth II (1953 - 1962)

This elegant early Elizabeth collection comes complete with four stylish red springback albums containing a space for every stamp and numerous illustrations throughout.

Queen Elizabeth II includes four springback albums, starter mount pack and over 400 unmounted mint stamps.

Queen Elizabeth II Only £595 or 5 payments of £119
(Retail value £700)

For further information please contact Mark Leonard on +44 (0)207 836 8444 or write to our London office

Stanley Gibbons
399 Strand, London, WC2R 0LX
Tel: +44 (0)207 836 8444
Fax: +44 (0)207 836 7342
Email: mailorder@stangiblondon.demon.co.uk
Internet: http://www.stangib.com